Perception and Understanding in Young Children

An Experimental Approach

Perception and Understanding in Young Children

An Experimental Approach

PETER BRYANT

Basic Books, Inc., Publishers

NEW YORK

Library of Congress Catalog Card Number: 73-92722
SBN: 465-05488-9
Printed in the United States of America
74 75 76 77 78   10 9 8 7 6 5 4 3 2 1

Contents

Foreword and Acknowledgements

Nowadays most books on psychology start with a *caveat* or two. I have a particularly pressing obligation to do so. The reader should be warned that this book is *not* a review. Although the book is based around the implications of some extremely well known developmental experiments, such as the conservation, the transposition and the transitivity experiments, I have not tried to cover the vast literature which exists on these different ways of looking at children's behaviour. Instead I have concentrated on the logic behind the design of these and other developmental experiments and have illustrated my argument with only a few key studies.

Inevitably some of my conclusions will be controversial, but perhaps this is not a bad thing. Fifteen years or so ago child psychology used to be a tranquil and also a relatively undervalued branch of psychology. Now the tranquillity has gone completely and at the same time the interest in children's behaviour has grown enormously. I think that these two changes go hand in hand. Having something to argue about is usually a sign of health in psychology.

Most of the argument which this book puts forward is the product of the research in which I have been involved over the past six years in Oxford. Very little of this research would have been possible without the help of my colleagues and friends, Jane Weightman, Pauline Jones, Vicky Claxton, Wendy Lawrensen, Cherie Bettison and Susan Martin. We had generous support from the Mental Health Research Fund, the Social Sciences Research Council and the Medical Research Council.

I was also extremely fortunate to have friends in the Department of Experimental Psychology at Oxford whose advice and criticisms were always acute and interesting. I am particularly grateful to Dick Passingham, Paul Harris and Jerome Bruner for having taken my ideas seriously, whether they agreed with me or not.

Then there is a former colleague of mine, Ati Hermelin, to whom I am indeed indebted. She read the manuscript of this book carefully and critically and her comments were incisive and, as always, most refreshing.

My wife Bridget also read the manuscript and gave me valuable help with comments which were intelligent, very perceptive and full of her usual sense of humour. She also corrected my English, read the proofs with me and generally made this book possible. I am very grateful.

I should like to thank the St John's College office for typing the manuscript.

Oxford July 1973

Perception and Understanding in Young Children

An Experimental Approach

I

Introduction

Our perception and our understanding of our environment are very closely linked, and this relationship between what we perceive and what we understand is almost certainly a two-way one. The better we understand the world around us, the more effectively can we set about gathering information about a particular part of it, and similarly the better we perceive our surroundings, the more efficiently can we interpret what is going on around us.

At no time in our lives is this connexion between perception and understanding more important than during childhood, because it is then that both undergo the most radical changes. Certainly it is during childhood that we lay the basis of our understanding of the rules which govern our environment. However imperfect our grasp of these rules as adults is, it is nonetheless the product of a very lengthy development. It is also fairly certain that there are greater changes in our perception during childhood than at any other time. Recent research, it is true, has established that even very young babies possess an impressive range of perceptual abilities (Kessen, Haith, and Salapatek, 1970). Nevertheless, it is still certain that these capacities alter, and generally become more effective, as children grow older.

How are these two types of development related? This is the question which prompts this book. The book's main aim is to present a theory about the way young children perceive their environment, and about how the perceptual information which they have to deal with affects their comprehension of the rules governing this environment. The theory itself is a limited one. It does not deal with all aspects of the young child's perception, but concentrates instead on the way children deal with recognizable perceptual continua, such as size, orientation, and position, and on the effects which their perception of these continua has on their understanding of such central notions as size, space and number.

The book then is not in any way a review. It concentrates on only some aspects of perceptual development, and on only one theoretical approach to a subject in which there have been many theories. The theory itself is based on the idea that an extremely important factor in the young child's perception of his world is his use of logical inferences to help him make perceptual judgements. The main argument will be that young children depend very heavily on inferences in making most of their important perceptual judgements, and that finding out about the reasons for this dependence and about the effects of these inferences can throw a great deal of light on the question of how children learn about their environment.

The theory is in some ways a novel one. Yet several of its ingredients are extremely familiar. Many of the ideas which are central to it were also discussed at length in some of the earliest and most important accounts of perceptual development. In particular, the perceptual theories of Helmholtz and of Piaget use the idea of perceptual inferences extensively, and the Gestalt theory of perception, although not directly concerned with the issue, did, it can be argued, establish one very good reason why inferences are necessary.

Perhaps the best way to approach the theory set forth in this book is to deal first with these more familiar accounts of perception, and to show how many of the ideas which occur in these can be incorporated, sometimes in a slightly altered form, in a new theory about perceptual development which can be used to explain a surprisingly wide range of recent experimental data on the behaviour of young children.

Perceptual inferences—the influence of Helmholtz

One of the earliest and also most influential theories about perception and perceptual development used as its central theme the suggestion that a great deal of what we perceive depends on our being able to make rapid and automatic inferences. This was the theory of H. von Helmholtz, the nineteenth-century German physicist and physiologist, who through his work on the sensory systems also became interested in the psychology of perception.

Helmholtz was impressed with the possibility that what a person perceives may be considerably affected by his past experiences. He argued that the sensory systems on their own are not versatile enough to account for the richness of perception, particularly of visual perception, and he suggested that people attain their perceptual sophistication by learning the meaning of particular cues in their environment. For example, the retina is two-dimensional, and yet we see things in three dimensions. Helmholtz put forward the idea that we are able to recognize the third dimension because we have learned to associate certain two-dimensional cues with depth. He further suggested that we use this learning inferentially. When we perceive cues which, for example, have in the past been associated with depth, we immediately infer that they signify depth once again.

These are 'unconscious inferences', which means that they are automatic, not expressed in words, and that the individual is not on the whole aware of making them. Yet they are nonetheless logical inferences. In one of his lectures Helmholtz described their logical status in the following way: 'There appears to me to be in reality only a superficial difference between the conclusions of logicians and those inductive conclusions of which we recognize the result in the conceptions we gain of the outer world through our sensations. The difference chiefly depends upon the former conclusions being capable of expression in words, while the latter are not: because instead of words they only deal with sensations and the memory of sensations' (Helmholtz, 1873).

Helmholtz even argued that in some ways these unconscious inferences are more powerful than inferences of which one is aware and which one can express in words. 'Just because they are not free acts of conscious thought these unconscious conclusions from analogy are irresistible, and the effects of them cannot be overcome by a better understanding of the real relations. It may be ever so clear how we get an idea of the luminous phenomena in the field of vision when pressure is exerted on the eye, and yet we cannot get rid of the conviction that this appearance of light is actually there at a given place in the visual field: and we cannot seem to comprehend that this is a luminous phenomenon at the place where the retina is stimulated' (Helmholtz, 1866). In his view, however conscious we might have been of the learning which established them, we are not aware of the perceptual inferences when we actually make them.

There are two main points which can be made about this theory. The first, and most frequently made, concerns his ideas about the role of experience in perceptual development. The second, which is far less commonly discussed, involves his notion of logical mechanisms in perception. Of these two points the first has very little bearing on the argument to be developed in this book, while the second is crucial to its hypothesis about perceptual development.

The basis for the first point is that these inferences are plainly inductive, and Helmholtz himself went to great lengths to emphasize this. An inductive inference is based on the assumption that a relationship which has existed in the past will continue to apply in the present. Thus one infers that a particular cue signals something because it has always signalled it in the past. Each inference then depends on the 'association of ideas going on in the dark background of our memory' (Helmholtz, 1894). Past experience is, therefore, crucially important, and if it affects perceptual inferences in this radical way, it must, if Helmoltz was right, also influence the way a person perceives.

This inductive aspect of Helmholtz's theory has attracted most attention, because it places him clearly in the familiar debate about whether perceptual abilities are innate or acquired. He is now chiefly remembered as an extreme empiricist by those who are interested in perceptual development, because the nativist–empiricist question, more than any other, has dominated this field of study throughout this century. It is true that he regarded very little in perception as innate, except, interestingly enough, the mechanism for making inferences. However, one's view of this side of Helmholtz's theory is bound to be coloured by one's opinion of the value of the nativist–empiricist debate. It could reasonably be argued that it is unfortunate that so much energy has been spent on the question of whether perceptual capacities have to be acquired, rather than on the equally interesting question of how children use them. And it is regrettable that the emphasis on Helmholtz's empiricism has been allowed to obscure the importance of the other side of his contribution – his interesting notion of logical mechanisms actively affecting what children and adults perceive. One particularly attractive feature of this idea is that it suggests a connexion between the way our immediate perception is organized and the way we organize our understanding of our world. What Helmholtz is saying is that we go through much the same processes when we judge, for example, the distance of an object as when we have to solve a logical problem. If this is so, then we should be able to use the results of perceptual experiments to help us understand something of the difficulties which people, and particularly children, have in logical problems, and vice versa. We should then be able to cross the divide usually found between experiments on perceptual development and experiments on cognitive development.

We are faced, then, with the conclusion that Helmholtz's general idea of logical mechanisms affecting perception and perceptual development was an important one, but that his particular emphasis on inductive inferences was probably unfortunate. This, of course, is no reason why the general idea should be abandoned. One perfectly valid way of pursuing his approach is to look for other logical manœuvres which might affect the young child's perception of his environment, and which might also be, in the Helmholtz manner, automatic and not expressed in words. Such logical mechanisms, as we shall see, are not hard to find. However, before going into the form they might take, we need to look at some aspects of another theory about perceptual development, which is also concerned with the possibility of logical manœuvres in perception. This is the theory of Jean Piaget.

Deductive inferences – the influence of Piaget

Not everyone ignored the logical side of Helmholtz's theory. The major exception was Jean Piaget, a Swiss psychologist, whose massive body of work on children is very well known. Piaget also recognized the importance of the idea that logical mechanisms might affect perception, and actually suggested new possibilities. One particular innovation in his theory of perceptual development, clearly described in his book *The Mechanisms of Perception* (1969), was the suggestion that at some stage in his life the child begins to use deductive inferences in order to make many of his perceptual judgements.

As is well known, Piaget's main interest in children has been their logical abilities; his general theory is that children only very gradually acquire the ability to be logical, and that logical development proceeds in several well-defined and ordered stages. A good example of his thought, and a pertinent one here, concerns the ability to make deductive inferences. These differ from the inductive inferences described by Helmholtz in that while the latter depend largely on experience with material at hand and on the assumption that past relationships will continue in the future, deductive inferences are quite independent of these conditions, and involve the use of a rule which can be applied to the familiar and to the unfamiliar equally conveniently.

A pertinent example, since it is an inference about a perceptual continuum, is the transitive deductive inference with which Piaget is most concerned. Suppose that we are shown first that $A > B$, and then quite separately that $B > C$. We can combine these two direct comparisons

to make a third, indirect and therefore inferential judgement that
A > C. Adults can make this transitive inference, but Piaget, on the
basis of experiments involving logical problems very like the one
described, argues that young children of less than eight years old
cannot (Piaget and Inhelder, 1941; Piaget, Inhelder, and Szeminska,
1960). He holds that below eight years children tend to be dominated
by their immediate perceptual input, and are quite unable to reorganize
it once it arrives. Their failure to produce the A > C inference is cited
as an example of how perceptual domination and logical ineptitude go
hand in hand in young children.

After this very brief account of Piaget's notions of children's inability
to make deductive inferences about continua, we can consider how he
relates it to the way in which they perceive. He makes two points:
first, that deductive inferences could be employed with great effect in
perceptual judgements about continua such as size and orientation,
and secondly, that young children do not employ them simply because
they cannot make this sort of inference before the age of about eight
years.

Piaget argues that deductive inferences affect our perception primarily
through the use of external frames of reference to connect and to
categorize separate perceptual experiences. For example, one way of
judging that the level of liquid in a glass always retains the same
orientation even though the glass itself is tilted from side to side, is by
noting that, whatever happens to the glass, the liquid's level always
parallels some external feature, like a table top. If A is the orientation
of the liquid at one time, and A_1 at another, and B is the table top, it
can be seen that A parallels B, that A_1 parallels B, and therefore A and
A_1 are in the same orientation. This is a deductive inference. In fact
Piaget argues that it is through making this kind of inference via an
external framework feature that children eventually come to understand that liquid levels stay horizontal (Piaget and Inhelder, 1956:
Piaget, 1969). However, his point here is a developmental one. Young
children cannot, he argues, use external reference frames in this inferential way until they are able to make deductive inferences.

One piece of evidence offered by Piaget for this developmental
change is drawn from an experiment in which he and his colleagues
gave young children an outline drawing of a bottle and a table top, and
asked them to draw a line to depict the level of the liquid in a real bottle
placed in front of them. Sometimes this bottle was upright, and at other
times tilted. It was found that five- and six-year-old children tended to

draw in the line in the right orientation when the bottle was upright, but as still perpendicular to its sides when it was tilted. This is a striking result, because the child is actually misrepresenting something which is there before him. Piaget concludes that these children did not yet know how to use the external reference system, and therefore did not understand that the level of liquid rests constantly horizontal. 'At the outset the child is not even aware of physical or physiological notions of vertical and horizontal, and for a very simple reason as these results show. The reason is that a perception only covers a very limited field, whereas a system of reference presumes operational co-ordination of several fields, one with another. Far from constituting the starting point of spatial awareness the frame of reference is the culminating point of the entire psychological development of Euclidean space . . .' (Piaget and Inhelder, 1956, p. 416).

Piaget later made a similar point about judgements of size (Piaget, 1969). If children are shown two sticks whose height is equal, but of which one is further away than the other, they typically judge the further one as smaller, an error sometimes referred to as a failure in size constancy. Piaget asked if they would stop making this error if the two stimuli were both compared to some common reference point. He and his colleague, Lambercier, showed children a nearer rod, A, and one farther away, C, whose size was the same, and compared each of them successively to another, moveable rod, B, again of the same size. They asked children general questions about the transitivity principle, and they also asked them to compare A and C after both had been shown B. They found that children in the five- to seven-year-old range did not seem to understand transitivity, and that showing them that both A and C equalled B did not reduce the extent to which they underestimated C. In the seven- to nine-year-old range they understood the transitivity principle, yet still continued to underestimate C. It was not until the age of nine to eleven years, which is quite old in developmental terms, that children appeared to begin to use the common reference point B to help them make the perceptual comparison between A and C at all systematically.

Piaget's conclusion from this result is that children have to grasp the logical principle first, which they do between seven and nine years, and then have to be thoroughly familiar with it before they allow it to influence their perceptual judgements. 'It must therefore be acknowledged that transitivity derives from sensory motor processes which are more general than the perceptual processes . . . and that it has repercussions upon perception instead of being derived from it' (Piaget, 1969, p. 336).

This is an important experiment because it illustrates extremely clearly Piaget's views on deductive inferences, use of external frameworks and perceptual development. If a child cannot make transitive deductive inferences, he cannot use external frames of reference, and he cannot therefore bring together and co-ordinate separate perceptual experiences in an effective and systematic way.

Later in this book it will be argued that children can actually make transitive inferences while still very young, and that they depend on external frameworks to a far greater extent than do older children and adults. Such a view is, of course, the direct inverse of Piaget's. However, notwithstanding this kind of disagreement, Piaget's idea of linking inferences and external frameworks as a vehicle for perceptual judgements is an important one, for several reasons. One is that it develops the most interesting part of Helmholtz's approach to perception and perceptual development by suggesting another way in which logical mechanisms can be used in perception. Another is that the inference with which we are now concerned, the deductive inference, has the advantage of being neutral as far as the innate-acquired hypothesis is concerned. To make a deductive inference properly the child does not have to be at all familiar with the specific material at hand. The actual ability to make deductive inferences may itself have to be acquired, but this is a separate question. A third reason is that Piaget's idea introduces the notion of the external framework as an important reference point through which separate perceptual experiences can be categorized. Finally the theory raises the possibility of developmental changes in the way logical mechanisms influence perception whereas Helmholtz assumed that children make their unconscious inferences in much the same way as adults.

This account of Piaget's theory about perceptual development is a very selective one. He saw the influence of inferences on children's perception as only one of the major factors in development; at one stage in *The Mechanisms of Perception* he lists fourteen major differences between 'perception' on the one hand and 'intelligence' on the other, and only one of these concerns inferences. (To contrast two such global concepts as 'perception' and 'intelligence' may seem rather unattractively arbitrary, but Piaget's distinction is a developmental one, since he is mainly comparing the way in which children take in perceptual information about their environment before and after they have developed some basic logical abilities.) This specific issue of perceptual inferences and external frameworks has been selected for its bearing on the theory to be outlined in this book.

This theory deals with the idea of deductive inferences and the use of perceptual frames of reference very extensively, and its major disagreement with Piaget will be about developmental changes. It will be argued that children make deductive inferences from a very early age, and that they use these deductive inferences and external frameworks very heavily. In fact it will be suggested that, where there are developmental changes, they are the opposite of those suggested by Piaget. Young children of three and four years initially rely very strongly on framework cues, and use them inferentially as an effective way of categorizing and learning from their perceptual experiences; as they grow older they begin to acquire other, more flexible, props, which I shall categorize as internal frameworks, to help them organize their perception. The strategy which Piaget saw as a culmination of perceptual development is, in this alternative view, a very basic perceptual strategy, whose effects are limited and rather haphazard, and which children already begin to abandon by the time they reach the age of about six years.

However, before describing this alternative theory and the arguments for taking the opposite point of view to Piaget's, it is necessary to examine one other major theory about perception, Gestalt theory, because some of its ideas illustrate very neatly the answer to a question not yet mentioned, that of *why* the child needs to make deductive inferences in order to make certain perceptual judgements about the world around him.

Gestalt theory and the question of absolute and relative codes

The discussion so far has been concerned mainly with the question of how children take in information about perceptual continua such as size and orientation. One question which needs to be asked about reactions to continua such as these is whether the values perceived and remembered are absolute or relative in nature. When someone takes in information about different sizes or orientations, or about different distances, numbers, brightnesses and textures, he can do so absolutely or relatively. For example, if he is shown two sticks together whose lengths are different, he can either register somehow that A is 8 inches and B 4 inches in length, or he can note that A is larger than B, or, even more specifically, that A is twice as large as B. In the first case he is using an absolute code, in the second and third a relative one. The two codes are not necessarily mutually exclusive, but they are different.

There is a more specific reason why the absolute-relative question is important for this discussion, and this concerns the use of deductive inferences in perception. Transitive inferences about points along a continuum are not necessary if the absolute values are known. Suppose, for example, that a child is shown three sticks in two separate pairs. First he sees A which is 8 inches in length compared directly with B whose length is 4 inches. Next he sees B compared with C which is 2 inches long. Finally he is asked which is the longer, A or C, but is not allowed to compare them directly. How can he answer the AC question? One way, already described, is to make a transitive deductive inference. However, this would be entirely unnecessary if the child or adult were able to remember the absolute values of A and C. But if the child were capable of taking in only relative values, the only way he could solve the AC problem would be by making a transitive deductive inference.

Exactly the same argument can be made about perception of orientation. As Piaget has noted, one way of remembering the orientation of the level of liquid in a glass is to note that it parallels the table top. This is a relative judgement, and it can be used to make a transitive inference that the level's orientation does not change when the glass is tilted in a different direction. But this inference is not necessary if one has an internal absolute category which will tell one that the level on the first and second occasion is horizontal. One simply knows, without the help of an inference, that both times the level was horizontal, and therefore unchanged.

It follows from this analysis that the question of whether children use absolute or relative codes is crucial for any discussion of the role of inferences in perceptual development. Fortunately there is now a great deal of information about this, most of which has been assembled in a valuable book by Reese (1968). The question was originally posed by the Gestalt psychologists in the early years of this century. Their interest in it had nothing directly to do with the subject of perceptual inferences. They raised the question because they were primarily concerned with the perception of pattern, and they were impressed by the fact that people can recognize patterns even when the absolute values of their individual components change radically, provided always that the relations between components remain constant. A tune is recognizable despite the fact that it is transposed to a different key. An outline shape is still the same shape even when its absolute size is doubled or trebled. Relations are perceived in spite of massive transpositions of absolute values, and from this the Gestalt psychologists argued that the primary units of perception are relational, and that absolute values are really rather unimportant.

This relative principle was thus an important part of their theory. The issue was most vigorously pursued by two of the best known of the Gestalt psychologists, Wolfgang Kohler and Max Wertheimer. It was Kohler (1918) who pioneered the classic transposition experiment, a learning experiment designed to test whether the subjects learned on an absolute or a relative basis. This experiment was carried out with a variety of animals and also with some young children. It was a learning experiment, involving discriminations along the continuum of either size or brightness. It always took the same form, which had two distinct stages. In the first stage, the animal or child was shown, over a series of trials, two sizes (or brightnesses), which we can call I and II, and was rewarded for choosing one of these, say the larger (II). This training stage continued until he had learned to choose this stimulus on every trial. Then followed the second – the test stage – in which he was shown two new sizes, II and III. One of these, II, had the same *absolute* value as the correct stimulus in the training pair, while the other, III, had the same *relative* value, being the larger.

The question then was which of the two new stimuli the subject would pick. The consistent result was that both animals and children responded in a relative manner. If they were trained to go to the larger size, they chose the larger of the new test pair, even though the alternative stimulus was the same in absolute terms as the originally correct size. Exactly the same pattern appeared in the brightness transposition experiments, and Kohler naturally concluded that the basic code was relative, that animals and young children did not pay much heed to absolute values, and probably could not take them in if they tried.

This conclusion, it should be noted, is still a controversial one. Fairly soon after Kohler's experimental results were published, other psychologists began to turn up instances in which animals and young children actually failed to 'transpose' relative responses to new pairs. The controversy and these further experiments will be described in the next chapter, together with some quite recent work which shows fairly conclusively that Kohler's original argument is substantially correct.

However, there is one general criticism which can be levelled at the Gestalt position on the absolute–relative question. This is simply that it does not stress the limitations of relative codes. Yet there can be very little doubt that relative codes have some distinct disadvantages, notably that they do not register much about individual stimuli. If a child who uses primarily a relative code is shown a single object, he will not ordinarily be able to remember much about for instance its absolute size, because he has no effective way of recording it. In fact, if he depends on registering relations, the only way he can remember its actual size, to compare it to other sizes, is to relate it to the size of some constant background feature (if one is available) and then to use this relation inferentially.

This weakness was disregarded by the Gestalt psychologists. They always emphasized the effectiveness of relative codes, and even went so far as to argue that these codes should be especially stressed in educational settings. Wertheimer, in particular, was strongly of the opinion that the child's perception of patterns and structure was something the teacher ignored at his peril. In one of his earlier papers (1912), he argued that there are many instances in which primitive people who cannot count further than two nevertheless manage to make number comparisons between groups of objects, not by checking off object against object, but on the basis of the internal relational structure of each group. He then extended this argument to cover the education of children in modern society by trying to show how educational methods which stress the structure of a problem are far superior to methods which ignore structure and which, in his terms, demand a blind solution. Wertheimer's actual observations of schoolchildren, best described in his book *Productive Thinking* (1961) and in the account of his last seminars by Luchins and Luchins (1970), are acute and extremely ingenious. I do not wish to dissent from his general view of the importance of relations, structure, and pattern. Nevertheless, there do seem to be some important instances where it would be valuable for a child to be able to remember absolute values, and where remembering only relations is very little help.

This conclusion is a general one. It applies as much to any other perceptual continuum as to size. Take, for example, the case of the child's learning the rule that the level of liquid stays in a constant orientation whatever the tilt of the container. The child who can code absolute orientation will notice on one occasion that the level is horizontal, on another horizontal, and on another still horizontal, and will eventually be able to conclude that the orientation does not change. On the other hand, the child who can only code the relative orientations of two lines will not be able to learn that the orientation is constant from separate presentations of the container of liquid, because he is unable to compare experiences which happen at different times.

The disadvantage of relative codes is, in general, that they do not on their own enable a child to connect his past with his present experience of perceptual continua. Dependence on these codes must therefore heavily restrict his chances to learn about his environment, unless he can find a way round the difficulty. One way of doing this is to make inferences with the help of an external framework. This is the starting point for the argument of this book, whose central theme will be that because young children rely on relative codes they have to depend on external frameworks, which they use inferentially in order to remember and to learn from their perceptual encounters with their environment.

The theory

The chapters which follow will all be based on this theory of how young children perceive and interpret their surroundings. They will contain the basic evidence for and against the theory. The purpose of this section is simply to provide a very brief, introductory outline of it.

Two very general points should first be made. The first is that the theory is based almost entirely on experimental evidence. The reason for this emphasis on experiments is that they do in fact provide the most precise evidence we have about children's perception and understanding. It is true that experiments with children have their weak points, of which one of the most worrying is that it is often difficult to be sure of a direct link between the child's behaviour in the experimental situation and in real life. However, I hope this book will help demonstrate how invaluable the experimental method is, provided it is used with caution.

The second point is that the theory is based mainly on experiments with children between the ages of three and eight years. There is nothing special about this particular range of ages. It was chosen only because most of the relevant evidence seems to rest on experiments with children just before and just after they have reached school age.

In fact much of the actual theory has already been set out, in a somewhat disjointed manner, in the foregoing discussion and it should already be clear that it is concerned with four main issues: the question of absolute and relative codes in children's perception, the limitations of relative codes, the use of external frameworks, and the influence of perceptual inferences.

(1) *Absolute and relative codes*

The starting point for the theory is that young children can on the whole register and remember relative values with great ease, but have problems in situations in which they must remember absolute values along any continuum. There is nothing intrinsically odd about this absolute-relative discrepancy, since it exists in much the same way in adults as well. However, there is a difference between children and adults, the sort of difference which is usually described as 'developmental'. Mainly, it is that adults do possess some absolute codes which children do not.

But it has been known for some time that adults also have some difficulty in remembering absolute values. There are a number of experiments on adults which demonstrate that there is usually a limit to the number of absolute values which can be remembered at any one time. These experiments are described by Miller (1956), Garner (1962), and Siegel and Siegel (1972). In them subjects are presented with a series of stimuli which differ in absolute value along a continuum like size (Eriksen and Hake, 1955), spatial position (Hake and Garner, 1951), loudness (Schipper, 1953), and pitch frequency (Pollack, 1952). Each value is presented on its own, and so can only be distinguished from the others on the basis of absolute properties. The subject's task is to recognize each value and distinguish it from the others. This turns out to be surprisingly difficult: people can usually manage to recognize and tell apart only between three and eight values. Above this limit they begin to make errors.

Thus the difficulty with absolute values may well be general, but just particularly pronounced in young children. It will be suggested that young children have considerable problems in understanding the rules governing their environment simply because they cannot remember the absolute properties of objects around them, and that as they grow older they begin to develop some strategies for coping with them. This 'absolute' development is never complete, and its extent varies between continua. However the development is important, and can be used to account for a great deal of the information which exists on children's dealings with orientation, position, and number.

The theory deals with this developmental change, but it also deals with the typical behaviour of the young child before the change occurs, at a time when he is still heavily dependent on relative codes. In fact the remaining three aspects of the theory are concerned with the difficulties which the child has then, and with how he tries to get round them before he develops the appropriate absolute codes.

(2) The limitations of relative codes

The basic weakness of relative codes is that they are only adequate for direct comparisons between objects presented simultaneously. How can this problem be overcome? One way round it is to develop an absolute code, and this seems to be the most effective solution. But from a developmental point of view this seems to take a long time. For some continua children are really quite old before they seem to acquire an effective absolute code, while for others it is possible that they never acquire such a code at all.

However there is another solution, widely used by young children, which is to plot not only relations between different objects, but also between objects and their frameworks, and to connect separately-presented objects through their common relations with the same framework. This is a relative, not an absolute, solution, and it leads to the next aspect of the theory.

(3) The importance of external frames of reference in perceptual development

Objects are never presented in complete isolation, except in the very rare case of luminous figures in an otherwise totally darkened room. In normal illumination any object will be surrounded by a frame of reference, and usually it can be related to parts of a continuum. For example, the orientation of the sides of a book lying on a table will either be parallel to the sides of the table top or not. Suppose that they are. The child who cannot plot absolute values will be able to see this and remember it.

The size of the book can also be related to the table in much the same way. Normally it will be smaller than the table top. It may also be the same size as some part of the pattern on the table cloth. The child who cannot use absolute values will be able to remember these relative sizes, even though he does not remember anything about the actual size of either the book or the table top.

The theory is, therefore, that the young child's perception and memory of individual objects will be heavily influenced by their relations to their surrounding frames of reference. However it is not claimed that this is characteristic only of children. 'Framework effects' are a familiar phenomenon in experimental work on perception in adults, and were clearly demonstrated some time ago, for example in judgements about orientation. If one has to set a luminous rod to true vertical when this rod is surrounded by a luminous square frame in an otherwise completely dark room, one's judgements tend to be influenced by the frame's orientation. If it is tilted, one tends to miss true vertical, and to set the rod in the same direction as the surrounding framework (Witkin, 1959). The degree of the error varies between people, and, interestingly, is greater in children than in adults. Very similar framework effects in adults have been shown in experiments on size judgements (Rock, 1970), which will be described more fully in a later chapter, and on movement judgements (Brown, 1931).

Thus adults also depend on frames of reference, quite possibly because they also to some extent do not possess effective absolute codes. The theory to be pursued in later chapters does not hold, therefore, that dependence on frameworks is in any way unique to young children, but that it is probably greater in them than in older children and adults, because, in general, the older one gets the less completely one has to rely purely on relative codes.

How does the use of external frameworks solve the problem of connecting past with present experiences? The answer is that it can help the child provided that he is capable of making a deductive inference.

(4) *Deductive inferences in perceptual development*

Let us return to the example of the book on the table. It is shown to the child with its sides parallel to those of the table. This book, A, is then removed, and two other books are put on the table. One, B, parallels the sides of the table top, T; the other, C, does not. The child has no absolute code, but he does have a relative code for orientation which tells him simply whether lines are parallel or not. How can he tell which of the two new books B and C is in the same orientation as that of the first book A?

The answer is obvious. He notes first that A parallels T and remembers this. Then he sees that B also parallels T, while C does not. Since A and B both parallel T, he can work out that they share the same orientation, and that A and C do not. He uses the external frame of reference to connect two successive experiences through deductive inference.

To some extent this is a new way of looking at framework effects. On the whole when psychologists have come across these effects, they appear to have been struck by their negative aspects. Their emphasis has been on the errors induced. But these frameworks also have a positive role. They act as a mediating link through which successive experiences can be linked.

One advantage of this theory is that although it is primarily about the way children deal with the problems of using mainly relative codes, it applies not only to behaviour traditionally regarded as perceptual, but also to behaviour usually described under quite different headings, to take an important example, a child's reaction to number. Number is a continuum, and therefore something about which conceivably one could make relative judgements without being able to take in absolute values. It turns out that young children actually do so, and this fact can be used most effectively to explain a great deal of existing information on the way they make number judgements, and on their behaviour in tests on understanding the invariance of number.

Indeed, this book will aim to provide a conceptual link between sets of experiments with young children which are usually treated quite separately. I shall try to show how experiments on absolute and relative learning, on the discrimination of mirror-images, on transitive inferences, on cross modal matching, on perceptual constancy and on conservation, experiments which are normally described under completely separate headings, may in fact be tackling very much the same problem from different angles. I shall also try to show that, taken together, the results of these apparently disparate sets of experiments become much more interesting and more valuable than when they are treated as dealing with separate issues.

2

Relations

The starting point for the theory just outlined is that young children depend primarily on relative codes. The first issue to be discussed is therefore the absolute–relative question. Is it true that young children take in and remember the relations between things fairly easily, but tend not to remember the absolute properties of individual objects? If it is, then at least one part of the theory is right. If it is not, and young children are found to take in absolute values very well, then the whole theory must be mistaken, since in that case children would need neither external frameworks nor deductive inferences to help them make perceptual judgements about continua.

The history of the work on the absolute–relative question is long and complex. Fortunately it has been comprehensively reviewed in two books, one by Reese (1968), the other by Riley (1968). This chapter will not, therefore, review all the experimental work, but will confine itself to giving an outline of the arguments which have arisen and the kinds of experiments which have been done in this area.

The first major step in the history of this problem was Kohler's attempt to settle the absolute–relative question by means of the trans-position experiment already described. All that remains to be said is that it was one of the very few experiments done by the Gestalt psychologists which used a learning task, and for this reason it attracted the attention of learning theorists in America much more than any of the other Gestalt experiments.

In particular Kohler's work on transposition interested the stimulus–response (S–R) learning theorists. This was not surprising, because one of the basic assumptions of the S–R approach was that animals record absolute values and do not, on the whole, respond to relations. Since their approach was the opposite of the Gestalt psychologists', they naturally felt they had to provide an answer to Kohler's apparently convincing and contrary results. Their experiments form the next major stage in the study of the absolute–relative problem.

S–R learning theory and the absolute–relative question

We owe S–R theory initially to Hull (1943), though it is Spence's extension of Hull's ideas to discrimination learning which will concern us most. Hull's main contention was that the basic unit of learning is a learned connexion between a specific stimulus and a specific response. This kind of analysis is usually applied to the way animals learn. The idea is that whenever an animal encounters a stimulus he retains a trace of this stimulus in his central nervous system. Also, whenever he makes a response to a stimulus he retains a trace of this response and of the stimulus to which the response was made, in the form of a stimulus–response (S–R) connexion.

The question then is how long this S–R trace will last, and what sorts of S–R traces will last longer than others. Hull's answer is well known. When a particular response to a particular stimulus is consistently followed by reward or reinforcement, that S–R trace lasts, and its continued existence ensures that the animal goes on making the same successful response to the stimulus on subsequent occasions. However, when the response is unsuccessful and is not consistently followed by a reinforcement, the S–R trace withers and fades, and is no longer effective.

The theory is one of the survival of the fittest S–R combinations. Those S–R connexions which tend to reduce the animal's needs are the ones which occur again, while those which are not so successful tend not to be repeated. The force which strengthens a S–R trace after a reinforcement is described as excitation, and the force which weakens the trace after non-reward as inhibition. These two forces are cumulative: the more often a particular S–R connexion is reinforced, the greater the excitation which builds up to it. Excitation and inhibition are also mutually antagonistic. Adding excitation to a particular S–R connexion wipes out some of the inhibition which might have been attached to it, and vice versa.

This approach to learning raises many interesting issues, of which only one will be discussed here. This concerns the nature of the way in which the animal stores the stimulus in the S–R trace. According to Hull, and later to Spence (1937, 1938), it is the absolute properties of the stimulus which are recorded. This absolute approach to learning can be illustrated most clearly by Spence's use of S–R theory to analyse the way an animal learns a simple discrimination task.

In discrimination tasks the animal is usually shown two stimuli on each trial, over a series of trials, and has to learn that responding to one of these leads to a reward, while responding to the other does not.

Usually the task continues until the animal reliably chooses the correct, rewarded stimulus on each trial. Suppose, for example, that in a discrimination task in which the correct and incorrect stimuli differ in size, the correct stimulus is a 6-inch square card, and the incorrect stimulus is a 3-inch square card. According to Spence, the animal stores these two absolute sizes, and builds up excitation to the S–R

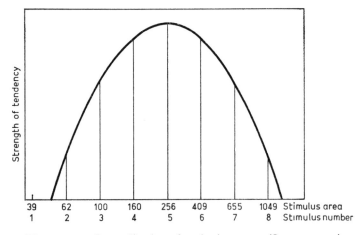

Figure 2.1 Generalization of excitation curve (Spence, 1937)

connexion which leads to an approach to the 6-inch square card, and inhibition to the connexion which involves an approach to the 3-inch square card. Excitation and inhibition are built up to specific and absolute values, and thus the animal learns to approach one absolute size and to avoid another. It learns nothing at all about the size relation. The fact that the correct card is larger is immaterial.

S–R theorists insisted on the specificity of the S–R connexions very firmly. It is true that they did admit that a response originally connected to one absolute value might also be made to other absolute values as well. This, however, was regarded as the product of the phenomenon of 'generalization', and generalization itself was thought to be based on absolute values. Spence (1937) in particular argued that the excitation or inhibition which was built up with one stimulus value would generalize to other values along the same continuum, but to a smaller and smaller extent the more the new values differed in absolute terms from the original value. Fig. 2.1 shows one of Spence's hypothetical generalization curves. Here he is suggesting what happens to excitation when an animal is originally trained to approach one particular size and then encounters other sizes. The area of the original stimulus is 256, and Fig. 2.1 shows that Spence thinks that most excitation is attached to this size. However he also thinks that when the animal subsequently encounters other sizes, these also arouse excitation, but to a lesser and lesser extent the further removed they are along the continuum. Thus more excitation is aroused by a 409 stimulus than a 655 one, because the former is nearer to the original stimulus than the latter.

This can only be an hypothesis, since excitation and inhibition are internal forces which are not directly observable, and it could very well be queried whether they really do exist. It is worth noting, however, that the hypothesis puts Spence's absolute notions in a rather strange position. The generalization takes place along a continuum, and thus the hypothesis is that animals can in some way recognize and use a continuum without being able to act on and recognize relations along that continuum. This seems paradoxical and somewhat improbable.

There was, therefore, a direct clash between the Gestalt theorists who claimed that relative codes are primary in animals as well as in man, and the S–R theorists who maintained that absolute codes were the basic ones. Obviously the S–R theorists had to find a way around the apparently clear relational effect in Kohler's transposition experiment. It was Spence who managed to suggest a way of explaining this result in absolute terms. He did so by demonstrating an effect called the distance effect, which certainly made the Gestalt position rather less secure, and on which most subsequent research in this area, including experiments on young children, has been based.

S–R transposition experiments and the distance effect

Kohler's transposition experiments always involved two pairs of stimuli only, the training pair and then the following transposition pair. Invariably the transposition pair was one ratio step along the continuum. Suppose that in the training pair one card is twice the size of the other. Then a pair one step away would consist of the larger of these first two cards together with a new card which was twice as large again. A pair two steps away would consist of the larger of the two cards in the second pair and another card twice as large, and so on. If Kohler is right in saying that the animal learns and transposes relations, it should not matter how many steps away from the original training pair the new transposition pair happens to be. A good test of the relative hypothesis, therefore, would be to extend Kohler's 'one-step' experiments by testing whether animals and young children also transpose relative responses to pairs which are several steps along the continuum.

The first person to look into the question of the 'distance' between the training and the test pairs was Kluver (1933), who in a size transposition experiment gave some monkeys two-and-a-half- and four-step transposition tests and compared performance on these tests with performance on the usual one-step transposition tests. He found that the animals which were given the one-step test, which has come to be known as the 'near' test, performed exactly as Kohler's animals had done: they made the relative choice. He also found that the other animals, who were given the 'far' tests, did not make the relative choice consistently, and that their performance was random in that it averaged out at chance level. Kluver's results were important, because they seemed to show that animals do not always transfer relations, and that their transfer performance is actually affected by the absolute differences between the training and the test pairs. However, his methods were a little too complex to make the interpretation of his experiments a simple one because he interposed some other learning tasks between training and test pairs.

Nevertheless, subsequent experiments seemed to confirm Kluver's conclusion that the distance between training and test pairs is indeed an important variable. Spence (1937) demonstrated that chimpanzees make less and less relative choices in a size transposition test the greater the difference between training and test pairs, and the distance effect was also observed in rats, both in size and in brightness transposition experiments (Maier, 1939; Kendler, 1950; Riley, 1958).

Two immediate points should be made about the distance effect. The first is that it is certainly difficult to explain on a purely relative hypothesis. There is nothing in the Gestalt analysis to account for a decline in the number of relative choices the greater the absolute distance between training and test pairs. It does seem, at first sight, that if the animal learns only relations he should act on these as consistently in the far tasks as in the near ones. The second point is that there is no direct evidence of an absolute response in these experiments. In the far tests, the animals did not consistently choose the absolute stimulus, i.e. the stimulus most like the initially correct stimulus in absolute terms. The most extreme effect of these far tests was to reduce the animals from relative to chance-level responding, and this means that although the absolute differences between training and test pairs does seem to mean something, distance does not itself induce overt absolute responding. These two points together seem to raise doubts about both hypotheses.

Spence's hypothesis about the generalization of excitation and inhibition

Spence however did not take such a pessimistic view about explaining these results in terms of a purely absolute code. He produced a remarkably ingenious hypothesis in terms of the generalization of the hypothetical forces, excitation and inhibition, which made it possible for

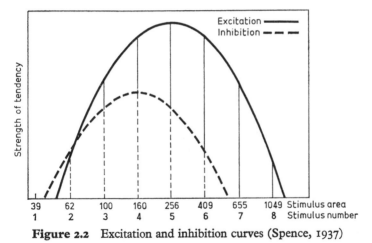

Figure 2.2 Excitation and inhibition curves (Spence, 1937)

him to dismiss Kohler's original one-step results as being pseudo-relative and the product of an absolute code.

Spence's analysis is best summarized in the curves presented in Fig. 2.2. These are generalization curves, and this time they depict the generalization of both the hypothetical forces, excitation and inhibition, which, according to S–R theory, are built up internally and attached to absolute stimulus values. In this example the continuum is size and the animal has been trained to respond to one size (256) and to avoid the other and smaller size (160). So excitation has built up to the larger of these and inhibition to the smaller. However both excitation and inhibition have generalized along the size continuum to other absolute values. There are two things to notice about these hypothetical curves. The first is that the continuum is plotted in logarithmic units: this is entirely appropriate since we are dealing with the effects of different ratio steps. The second is that the peak strength of inhibition is never as great as that of excitation, and the inhibition generalization curve therefore falls off faster than the excitation curve. This difference reflects a basic assumption of Hull's and Spence's approach, that if an S–R combination is followed as often by non-reinforcement as by reinforcement, the strength of its excitation will override that of its inhibition.

As we have seen in the S–R analysis the likelihood that a particular response will be repeated is determined by *net excitation* (that is to say, the degrees to which excitation exceeds inhibition) attached to the appropriate S–R connexion. In Fig. 2.2 the amount of net excitation attached to each point of the continuum after learning to approach the 256 stimulus and to avoid the 160 stimulus is indicated by the vertical lines. The whole point of Spence's analysis lies in the suggestion that the greatest *net* excitation belongs not to the initially correct value but to values further removed along the continuum in the positive direction, that is to say, away from the initially incorrect value. The reason for this rather surprising effect is that both excitation and inhibition generalize to the stimulus (409) which is one step along the continuum from the initially correct value, and that on the other hand this new stimulus is very much less affected by the generalization of inhibition, which is falling off very rapidly, than by the generalization of excitation.

The conclusion of this analysis, which is based entirely on the idea of an absolute code, is that if the animal is given a one-step test involving stimuli 256 and 409, it will again select the larger of the two (409) and will not pick 256, the previously correct value. Thus even though the animal is using only an absolute code it will respond to the one-step pair in an apparently relative manner.

This analysis may seem to be very laborious, and it is easy to sympathize with one author (Humphrey, 1951) who characterized it as 'grotesquely ponderous'. Certainly the theory seems rather artificial when one considers that there is no direct evidence at all for these hypothetical excitation and inhibition curves. Nevertheless the hypothesis does make some definite predictions about the effects of giving transposition tests far down the continuum, and so does provide a new basis for looking at the distance effect.

A glance at Spence's curves will show that the tendency to choose the same relative size as in the initial training pair should vary greatly as one moves further down the continuum. Animals originally trained to respond to the larger of the two stimuli with the pair 160 and 256 will definitely go on responding to the larger with the one-step test pair, 256 and 409. However the more steps one takes along the continuum the less likely it is that the same 'relative' choice of the larger one will be made, and with the three-step transposition tests the position is actually reversed, and the animals having originally learned to go to the larger of the two should, in these 'far' tests consistently choose the smaller size. Two predictions follow from this. The first is that the original tendency to make a relative response in near tests – in his terms a pseudo-relative response – will decline the further removed down the continuum the transposition test is. The second prediction is that at a certain point on the continuum there will be a 'transposition reversal', and the animal will begin to select the stimulus which is most similar to the originally correct one in absolute terms.

It is important to stress that although the first of these two predictions has ample support, the second prediction of a transposition reversal has not been found to be typical. The typical pattern is of a decline to chance level performance as one moves the transposition test further along the continuum. Although some authors write as though the transposition reversal was a reliable effect it is in fact a myth. Nobody has ever shown that animals can be made to respond absolutely by giving them far tests. The furthest they ever get from responding relatively in a far test is to behave randomly. On the whole this difficulty for Spence's theory was ignored by others working in this field, and many people came to assume that the distance effect was an unambiguous sign of absolute responding.

The distance effect and young children

Once the distance effect had been established with a wide variety of animals, psychologists naturally began to ask if it could also be found with humans as well, and as naturally began by looking for the effect with the least sophisticated humans available, young children. The original distance-effect experiment with children was carried out by Kuenne (1946) and the children whom she saw were all between the ages of four and eight years. Her experiment involved size transposition. Each child initially learned over a series of trials to choose one of a pair of white squares placed before him on a desk. The squares differed only in size, and once the child had learned the initial size discrimination he was given ten trials on either a one-step or a five-step transposition test. The children were put into various age groups from four to eight years, and while half of each age group was given the near test the other half was given the far test. The experiment was designed to test whether the extent of the distance effect changes as children grow older.

The experiment showed a clear difference between younger and older children. The youngest children showed a very strong distance effect. They made the relative choice in the near, one-step test very consistently, as is usual. However in the far, five-step test their performance was at 50 per cent chance level. The oldest age group, on the other hand, consistently made the relative response in both tests, and made it as strongly in the far test as in the near test. Thus the difference between the four- and the eight-year-olds was in their performance in the far test, and this trend was reflected in the scores of the intermediate age group. In other words, the distance effect declines with age. This pattern of results seems reliable. It was repeated in another developmental study by Alberts and Ehrenfreund (1951), and, as we shall see, other psychologists have confirmed the existence of a strong distance effect in four-year-old children.

Kuenne accepted the argument that the distance effect signifies an absolute code and she therefore argued that the clear age difference that had emerged in her study meant an absolute to relative developmental change. Her idea was that the four-year-old children took in only absolute sizes, and therefore did not transpose a relation to the far test. She went on to argue that as children grow older they become more and more capable of using a relative code.

She also had a suggestion for the cause of this apparent developmental switch from absolute to relative codes. Her hypothesis was that it was due to the development of language. She argued very simply that older children eventually manage to take in and use relations because they learn the appropriate relative words. They can transfer a response to the larger of two sizes because they can say to themselves while they learn the initial task that the 'larger' is the correct one. Younger children do not have these verbal labels readily to hand, and as a result behave in much the same way as do Spence's chimpanzees, Kluver's monkeys and Kendler's rats, which are also 'non-verbal'.

Kuenne's experiment was an impressive one, and in its way has become a classic study. However one can make at least two major criticisms of her conclusions. The first concerns her idea about the effects of language, and the second her interpretation of the distance effect as a sure sign of an absolute code. The main trouble with the hypothesis that children begin to take in and use relations to help them solve problems because they learn the appropriate comparative terms like 'larger' is that it leaves unanswered the very awkward question of how they learned the meaning of these words in the first place. If a child at first only takes in absolute values, he will have no basis for understanding the meaning of relational words when he first begins to hear them.

It is therefore very difficult to see how Kuenne's simple idea of the complete dependence of relative codes on language could work, and it is worth noting that her experiment does nothing in itself to demonstrate that language does play a part in the developmental changes which she found. It is true that the older children speak more and handle relational words better than younger children, and indeed Kuenne did, on the whole, show that the more children used verbal terms overtly the more likely they were to respond relatively in the far test. However one cannot infer a cause from this relation with language. There are many other differences between older and younger children than verbal ones, and any of these could have led to the fact that the distance effect was found with younger children but not with older ones.

Kuenne's second interpretation, based on the decline in the distance effect with age, that four-year-old children take in absolute values while eight-year-old children act on relative values, raises the crucial question of what the distance effect really means. At its most extreme in the four-year-old group, this effect took the form of high relative responding in the near test and chance level performance in the far test. It has already been suggested that this chance level behaviour in far tests is rather difficult to interpret, for two reasons. The first is that chance level performance does not demonstrate the *presence* of an *absolute* code, because random behaviour never definitely demonstrates the presence of any code at all. It is important to realize in research with children that chance level performance is always ambiguous. The child could be upset, distracted or thinking about his lunch when he is behaving randomly, and there is no reason to think that he must be coding absolute values.

The second point is that there is no reason to think that chance level performance in the far test indicates the *absence* of a *relative* code. Indeed one can put forward the counter argument that the distance effect is the result of the child taking in altogether too many relations rather than taking in none at all. The initial pair of stimuli used in the training stage of the transposition experiment are characterized not only by the relation between them, but also by the relation between them and their own surrounding background, a point which is largely owed to the work of Riley (1958) with rats. For example, Kuenne presented her white squares on the dark background of a desk whose size was constant. When the initial training pair was large the two squares together took up most of the desk, and a one-step transposition pair also took up an appreciable proportion of the desk, since their sizes were not all that different from those of the original training pair. On the other hand the squares in the five-step far test would have been very small indeed and would, therefore, only have taken up a very small proportion of the desk. Thus the second relation, the relation between stimuli and their background, changes much more radically between training and the far transposition test than it does between training and the near test.

It follows that another, and quite plausible, interpretation of the distance effect in young children is that in the initial task they take in two sorts of relations, the relation between the two stimuli and the relation between the two stimuli and their background. From the point of view of the task which has been set them, the first is the relevant and the second the irrelevant relation. When they are given the near transposition task they transfer the relevant relation with not much difficulty, since there has been very little appreciable alteration in the other type of relation. However in the far test they notice that the relation between stimuli and their background has undergone a drastic change, and uncertain what this change means, young children revert to behaving randomly.

This is a relative hypothesis, and yet it is also an alternative explanation of the distance effect. If it is right, Kuenne's general idea of an absolute to relative development is wrong. According to this alternative hypothesis the young child basically takes in relations and not absolute values, and the only developmental change is that the older children manage somehow to avoid being influenced by the irrelevant relations with the external framework. We must ask then whether there is any further evidence on the distance effect which supports this alternative approach.

Further experiments on the distance effect

There is some very good evidence that humans are strongly affected by background cues when they have to judge size. Rock and Ebenholtz (1959) asked adults to compare the lengths of two vertical luminous lines when these lines were surrounded by luminous rectangular frameworks of different sizes in an otherwise dark room. They found that their subjects were heavily influenced by the relation of each line to its own background, underestimating, for example, the length of the line in the larger framework, even when they were instructed to ignore these background cues. However these experiments, which will be described in some detail in Chapter 6, were not transposition experiments.

The clearest evidence for background effects in transposition experiments is provided by an experiment by Riley (1958) on the transposition of brightness. Riley specifically looked at the influence of cues in the background in this experiment, which was with rats. He trained his animals to respond to the lighter of two patches of light. Then he gave half of them a near and half a far transposition test in the traditional manner. However he also subdivided the near and far groups. For half of each group the background illumination was kept unchanged throughout the experiment, the typical transposition procedure.

However the remaining animals were treated differently. For them the background illumination was kept in a constant relation to the two brightnesses which had to be discriminated, so that if the two patches were fairly bright the background illumination was bright also while if they were dim, the background illumination was low. What happened in this experiment was that the distance effect occurred with the rats which were treated in the conventional manner with an unchanged background, but not with the rats for which the background illumination varied proportionally with the brightness of the stimuli that had to be discriminated. These latter animals responded relatively at a very high level in both transposition tests and made as many relative choices in the far as in the near test. This definitely seems to suggest that rats take in two sorts of relations when they learn the initial brightness discrimination, the relevant relation between the stimuli and also the irrelevant relation between the stimuli and their background. It seems that it is the marked change in the second kind of relation that leads to the disruption of performance in the far test and therefore to the distance effect.

The question which now arises is whether background cues also lead to the distance effect in children. As far as I know there are no direct tests of this idea with young children. There are, however, two excellent experiments by Johnson and Zara (1960) and by Sherman and Strunk (1964), which use a technique known as 'double discrimination' and which, it will be argued, fit in very well with the idea of young children using the background framework relatively in size transposition experiments. These experiments were not actually designed to test the framework hypothesis. However they can be explained by this hypothesis very neatly indeed.

Johnson and Zara's experiment was on size transposition by four-year-old children, and the new feature of this experiment was to make some children learn the initial training task with two pairs rather than with one. In the initial task they used four sizes with this new double-discrimination technique, and these, arranged in the usual ratio steps, were 1, 2, 3, and 4. Half the children learned the double discrimination, and they were given stimuli 1 and 2 on half the trials and 3 and 4 on the other half, the two pairs being presented in an interleaved and randomized way on the different trials in this task. They always had to make the same relative choice with both pairs so that if the larger was the correct choice in one pair it was also always the correct choice in the other. The other half of the children were given only a single pair during the initial training, and they always learned with the sizes 3 and 4 only. All the children, once they had learned the first task, were given ten trials in a transposition test. A third of the children in each group were given a one-step test involving 4 with 5, a third a two-step test 5 with 6, and the remaining third a three-step test 6 with 7.

The experiment produced two major results. First the single discrimination group showed the usual distance effect. They produced a high number of relative responses in the one-step test, but in the two- and three-step tests their performance was down to the chance level. Secondly there was no sign of a distance effect in the double-discrimination group who made as many relative choices in the two- and three-step tests as in the near one-step test. We now have for the first time an example of four-year-old children making very consistent relative choices even in a transposition pair some way down a continuum from the original training pair.

This experiment has been repeated with the same pattern of results by Sherman and Strunk (1964). These results have a strong bearing on the argument about the relative use of framework cues being put forward in this chapter. My suggestion has been that the distance effect is normally caused by the child's originally taking in background relations, despite the fact that these, strictly speaking, are superfluous to the task. Now one feature of the double-discrimination task is that the background relations must vary from pair to pair. The background relations for the pair containing 1 and 2 and for the pair involving 3 and 4 differ markedly, and it may be that the child given the double-discrimination task is being taught not only that the relation between the two stimuli in each pair is relevant, but also that the relation between stimuli and background is irrelevant since it varies from trial to trial. For the single-discrimination group, on the other hand, the background relations are constant throughout the training task and so this group is not taught to attend to one relation and to ignore the other.

This framework explanation of why the single-discrimination group shows the distance effect and the double-discrimination group does not is purely hypothetical, and is not the explanation offered by the experimenters themselves, who talk in more global terms of attentional variables. However, it has the advantage of linking some rather disparate transposition experiments, and it also provides a very good connexion with still other experiments. As will be shown in later chapters, the idea of children depending on background relations can be used to explain a very wide range of evidence on perceptual development.

However, one can also reach some firmer and less controversial conclusions from these important double-discrimination experiments. The first is that they make Kuenne's verbal mediation hypothesis even more doubtful. The manoeuvre which eliminates the distance effect, the introduction of a double discrimination, is essentially a non-verbal manoeuvre, and there seems to be no reason at all, on a verbal hypothesis, why it should produce such obviously consistent relational responding. The second conclusion is that even if one does not agree with the framework suggestion, these experiments raise once again the awkward question of whether the distance effect does mean an absolute code. If the distance effect is due to an absolute change between training and test stimuli, it is very difficult to see why this absolute effect did not apply also to the double-discrimination group. Simply to show that children do not in some instances respond relatively is very tenuous evidence for an absolute code.

Perhaps instead the question ought to be turned on its head. In the evidence presented so far psychologists have asked whether relative responding occurs, and have based their hypotheses about absolute codes on cases where it does not. Why not instead ask directly if children can respond absolutely, and whether, for example, they can solve a problem which demands that they take in and remember absolute values of one sort or another?

A direct comparison between absolute and relative tasks

Despite the complexities of the transposition experiments the basic questions behind the absolute-relative problem are still very simple. There are really two main questions. The first is whether young children can take in and use relations. The second is whether they can code absolute values. The experiments which have been described so far give a partial answer to the first question and no answer at all to the second. We have seen that in some circumstances, as for example, after learning a double discrimination, young children definitely do use a relational code, though there are signs that in other situations this code does not seem to be so effective. However, we have met no direct evidence at all that young children can take in absolute values. The data does not allow us to hazard even a guess whether or not young children use an absolute or a relative code more readily.

The only way to resolve this question would be an experiment which made a direct comparison between an 'absolute' task which could be solved only by using an absolute code, and a 'relative' task which could be solved only by using a relative code. Such an experiment would involve two kinds of tasks, one in which the absolute value of the correct stimulus is always the same, though its relative value changes from trial to trial, the other in which the correct stimulus always has the same relative value, even though its absolute value changes over trials. The first of these two tasks would be the absolute one and the second the relative one. The important questions are which of the two tasks is more easily learned, and whether the absolute task can be learned at all.

There have been several attempts to make this sort of direct comparison between absolute and relative size tasks in animals (Meyer, 1964; McCulloch, 1935), and one study has also made the same kind of comparison with children. This was an experiment by Graham, Ernhart, Craft, and Berman (1964). They worked with children aged between two and a half and four years and they gave some of these children absolute and others relative size-discrimination tasks. These tasks consisted of a series of trials in which each child was shown a pair of white squares whose sizes were different. The children had to learn to identify which of the two was the correct and rewarded one, and they could only do so on the basis of information about size. However, the actual sizes involved varied from pair to pair and thus from trial to trial. All pairs invariably contained one square with sides of 7·35 cm in length. However, the size of the other square varied from pair to pair, and was sometimes larger and sometimes smaller.

The correct and rewarded card always had the same absolute size (7.35 cm) for the children who were given the *absolute* task, but was sometimes larger and sometimes smaller than the incorrect card. For the children who were given the *relative* task, on the other hand, the correct card always had the same relative size on each trial, i.e. it was always the smaller or the larger of each pair. This meant that the absolute size of the correct square varied over trials. For example, the square with sides 7·35 cm long would be correct on some trials and incorrect on others, because sometimes it would be the smaller and sometimes the larger in the pair.

The result of this experiment was that children found the relative task much easier than the absolute one. They were, it seems, much better equipped to remember and to use a relation than an absolute value. This result seems to support the relative hypothesis.

There is, however, a difficulty about this interpretation, which is that Graham *et al.* had no control in their relative tasks for pseudo-relative responding of the type suggested by S–R theory. These relative tasks effectively only involve one-step differences, because all the pairs used in these tasks have one absolute size in common. The two pairs in Kohler's experiments and in Spence's and Kuenne's 'near' pairs also had one absolute size in common, and no one disputes that children and animals continue to respond to the same relative size when they are given this sort of combination of pairs. This means that the Graham *et al.* result could be explained in terms of the Spence generalization curves as a pseudo-relative response. The only way to obviate this is to set up a 'far' relative task in which the absolute values in one pair are quite different from those in the other, being several steps along the continuum.

We have recently carried out an experiment with four- and six-year-old children which compares absolute with relative tasks and which includes this type of control (Lawrenson and Bryant, 1972). Three main groups, an 'absolute', a 'relative', and a 'standard' group were tested. The absolute and relative groups learned tasks which were rather like the corresponding tasks in the Graham *et al.* experiment. These involved two pairs of white squares of different sizes, and the absolute tasks could be solved on the basis either of the correct or of the incorrect square always being the same actual size, even though its relation to the other square varied. In the relative tasks the situation was quite the opposite. The relative value of the correct and incorrect squares stayed the same for each child who was given this task, some children having to learn to respond to the larger the others to the smaller.

Thus far the technique is very similar to that of the Graham *et al.* experiment. Where it begins to differ is in having two types of relative tasks, a near and a far one. In the near test the two pairs were one step along the continuum from each other. In the far test one pair was five steps away from the other. Half the relative group learned one of these tasks, and half the other. Kuenne's experiment also used one- and five-step tests, and the actual sizes in our experiments were exactly the same as hers. The other main difference was that we included a standard group who were given only one pair of sizes. They could learn this task either on an absolute or on a relative basis and its purpose was to provide a baseline against which to compare the other two tasks.

This experiment produced five clear results: (1) The relative task was very much easier than the absolute task both for four- and for six-year-old children. Both age groups made more errors in the absolute task than in the relative task. (2) There was no difference between the near and far relative tasks, and thus no distance effect. (3) There was no significant difference between the relative and the standard groups. However the standard group made less errors and learned more successfully than the absolute group. (4) It made no difference within the absolute group whether it was the correct or the incorrect stimulus which always had the same absolute size. In both cases children had great difficulty in learning what to do, and often did not manage to learn at all. (5) There were no important differences between four- and six-year-old children in this experiment. The six-year-olds, as might be expected, seemed to do generally better, but the pattern of their scores was much the same as that of the four-year-olds.

These results are very strong evidence for the hypothesis that young children rely primarily on relative codes and have great difficulty when they are required to register absolute values. There does not seem to be any way in which this evidence can be explained by an absolute to relative developmental hypothesis. An absolute to relative hypothesis would have to predict that young children would have little difficulty with the absolute tasks but would be very slow indeed with the relative tasks, particularly with the far version of this task. There was no sign in this experiment of any difference between near and far relative tasks; this suggests that the distance effect will only be found in a traditional transposition experiment which comprises two very clearly demarcated stages, the training and test stages, and in which the child is aware of an abrupt change between the two stages. It is this abrupt change which, for the reasons already described, can bewilder the child and reduce him to chance-level performance. Our experiment, on the other hand, involved only one task, and therefore only one stage, for each child, and in it distance had no effect whatsoever.

The strengths and weaknesses of relative codes

The evidence suggests very strongly that relative codes are primary for young children. The experiments deal only with one continuum, that of size, but later chapters will describe experiments about others such as orientation, position and number, which point in the same direction.

What exactly are these size relations which four-year-old children are able to remember and to use with such ease ? One certainty is that they are able to recognize broad relationships, such as 'larger' and 'smaller'. These relationships are broad because they can be applied to any pair of stimuli whose sizes are different. Another possibility is that they can also recognize more specific relationships, such as size ratios, which apply to only some pairs of sizes, and this possibility is strongly suggested by our analysis of the traditional distance effect. If it is true that children are confused in far tests by an abrupt change in the relation between the stimulus and its background, they must be coding some kind of a ratio. The size of the background is always greater than the size of the stimuli, however different the stimulus pairs are from each other. The change in the relations between stimuli and background which takes place when the child is switched from the training to the test pair is a ratio change. However, this idea about ratios is, at the present stage of the argument, a very tentative one. It will be taken up again in Chapter 6. At the moment all that can be said definitely is that children can respond to the categories of 'larger' and 'smaller', and have difficulty in remembering absolute values.

Nevertheless this conclusion is a reasonable start for the theory being developed, and since one important aspect of this theory is that relative codes have their disadvantages, we ought now to consider what these disadvantages are. If a child can remember a relation such as 'larger' but cannot remember anything effective about the absolute sizes of the squares which he sees, he is obviously going to be in difficulties when he encounters one square at a time. If he cannot remember the actual size of a square which he has seen time and time again, he is obviously not going to benefit much from specific experiences with specific sizes, and will therefore be handicapped in his efforts to categorize his experiences with the size dimension.

This is a point which has been ignored by most of the people involved at one time or another in the transposition issue. Certainly there is no hint at all in the transposition papers written from an S–R point of view either that a relative code might constitute a rather limited way of taking in information about the environment, or that an absolute code might in any way be a sophisticated one. The reason for this is that one of the major aims of S–R learning theory was to show that the basic unit of learning, the S–R connexion, is highly specific. Relations are not specific in that they can be applied to an infinite number of stimuli along the continuum, and so from the S–R point of view relative codes are complex and sophisticated, and therefore unlikely to be found either in animals or in young children. The argument is a reasonable one, but it is only reasonable if one first accepts the premise that the basic unit of learning is the specific S–R connexion which is based on the absolute value of S. Since it seems that children have great difficulty in remembering absolute sizes, it is most unlikely that their behaviour, at least when they deal with sizes, can be explained in terms of S–R units.

In fact, common sense also tells us that we tend to concentrate on relative values and to ignore absolutes when we can. Very few of us for example have perfect pitch. We can tell whether two sounds presented fairly soon after one another have the same frequency or not, but we cannot normally recognize and tell apart a whole range of individual tones on the basis of their absolute frequencies. Significantly we regard people who have perfect pitch and can assign absolute values to individual tones as highly sophisticated. Nobody dismisses their achievement as a basic S–R phenomenon. The absolute judgement experiments on adults described in the last chapter support this point of view, and it would be interesting to know how young children would fare if they were given this kind of task. It is almost inconceivable that they would manage any better than an adult does, and one could with some confidence hazard the guess that they would do a great deal worse.

We are left with the question of how children manage to get around the difficulties which they have with absolute values. In the next three chapters I shall present detailed evidence for the hypothesis that the child's basic tool for organizing his perceptual experiences and learning from them is the deductive inference.

3

Inferences

The discovery that the young child is able to handle size relations fairly efficiently naturally leads one to speculate whether or not he can also combine these relations in an inference. Obviously he can register that A is larger than B and that B is larger than C. Can he then go on to work out that this means that A must be larger than C?

The argument which has been developed, and which was outlined initially at the end of the first chapter, is that the young child is able to co-ordinate relations and that this difficulty with absolute judgements makes it a particularly urgent matter that he should. His weakness at remembering absolute properties forces him to put separate relative judgements together to produce deductive inferences.

This is a simple idea, but it is also extremely controversial. The suggestion that children can make deductive inferences goes directly against many influential accounts of children's behaviour. In particular, it disagrees with hypotheses put forward by Piaget (1970), and by Kendler and Kendler (1967), which suggest that children are not able to co-ordinate separate judgements inferentially until they reach the age of roughly seven or eight years.

Piaget, for example, in a recent publication (1970) writes about his approach to the question of inferential ability in the following terms: 'We present two sticks to a child, stick A being smaller than stick B. Then we hide stick A and show him stick B together with a larger stick C. Then we ask him how A and C compare. Pre-operational children will say that they do not know because they have not seen them together – they have not been able to compare them.' Thus, to Piaget it seems that the young perceptually dominated child cannot compare things unless they are presented together in one perceptual event. Separate perceptual experiences can never be combined, and no deductive inference is possible.

The Kendlers, whose background is that of the American school of S-R learning theory and very different from Piaget's, draw conclusions about inferential abilities which are at least as pessimistic as his. Thus they end a review (1967) in the following way. 'Investigators have shown that rats do not solve problems that require the integration of separate habit segments. There may even be some question of whether infra-human primates would be able to solve such problems, given appropriate experimental controls. When a similar experimental paradigm is applied to a cross section of human beings we find that if we use either grade level or M.A. as a developmental index solutions are very infrequent at the lower developmental levels. However, as developmental level increases solutions become increasingly frequent until at the highest level they are over-whelmingly the dominant mode of response. . . . Children at the lower developmental levels do not integrate the two segments at the first opportunity because they have learned to make different responses to these compounds.' Thus, the Kendlers' opinion is that young children are as incapable as rats at making inferences, and may even be worse than monkeys or chimpanzees.

This disagreement between my theory that deductive inferences are a very basic part of the young child's behaviour and the theories of Piaget and the Kendlers, which claim that young children cannot make inferences, suggests that the evidence on the inference question should be very carefully examined. There is also another reason why this issue is important, and that is its educational significance. A child who cannot put together the information that A > B and B > C to produce the inference that A > C clearly cannot understand even the most basic principles involved in measuring things. There will be little point, for example, in teaching such a child to use a ruler, because he will have no conception that different things could be compared with each other through their common relations to it. If, on the other hand, he can make inferences, this opens up educational possibilities for young children which may be of considerable benefit to them.

What, then, is the evidence for and against the proposition that young children can and do make deductive inferences? An examination of this evidence raises some intriguing problems to do with experimental design. The question is a delicate one, and the right controls are all-important.

Piaget and the transitivity problem

Piaget's original experiments on the way children cope with inference problems (Piaget and Inhelder, 1941, Chaps. 10 and 11; Piaget, Inhelder and Szeminska, 1960) took the form of his three-sticks example which has just been described. These experiments, which he and his colleagues called 'transitivity' experiments, involved either different sizes or different weights, and they consisted of three separate stages. First two quantities would be directly compared, A with B. Then one of these quantities, B, would be directly compared to a third, B with C. Finally, the child would be asked about the relations between the two quantities which he had not compared directly, A with C. This last stage presents the inferential problem, since in order to answer the AC question the child must combine the information from the separate direct comparisons between A and B and between B and C.

What happened in these experiments was that children below the age of approximately seven or eight years were not able to answer the inferential AC question. Above this age children generally did manage to make the inference satisfactorily. These results were consistent across several different experiments, and many other psychologists, who have repeated Piaget's three-stage transitivity experiment, have come up with the same developmental trend from consistent failure to consistent success. The most notable example is Smedslund (1963, 1966) who has done an interesting series of variations on Piaget's original experimental design and has arrived at much the same conclusions.

One of Smedslund's ingenious inferential tests is well worth describing at this point (Smedslund, 1966). The experiment was with children aged from five to seven years and again the problem was whether they could work out that $A > C$ from the information that $A > B$ and that $B > C$. The striking feature of this test, which forms only one condition in a rather complex experiment, was that the rods A and C were presented together and side by side, and were actually the same size. They were black rods, both 20 cm in length. The trick of the experiment was to have two B rods, both yellow, and yet to convince the child that there was only one B. One of the two Bs was 19·5 cm and the other 20·5 cm. The child was shown first that A was longer than B using the shorter B and next that B was longer than C using the longer B. The child, who was meant not to be aware of the switch from one B to the other, then had to work out which was the longer, A or C.

The advantage of making A and C the same length is that it gets round the difficulty of the children solving the problem, not inferentially, but simply by remembering the actual lengths. If the child is shown, for example, first a 21 cm A with a 20 cm B, and next a 20 cm B with a 19 cm C, he could perhaps solve the AC problem not by combining the two judgements inferentially but merely by remembering that A was 21 cm and that C was 19 cm. Simply remembering the absolute lengths does not involve an inference.

In fact, the experiment which included this test of what Smedslund called 'genuine measurement' produced no evidence that children below eight years were able to make transitive, deductive inferences, and Smedslund concluded that his results were very much in line with Piaget's suggestions. There is one unsatisfactory detail about this experiment. It is not at all clear why, if children could register the absolute lengths of A and C, they could not also remember the absolute lengths of the two Bs and thus realize that they had been fooled. If the control were really necessary, the test would be a bad one because children who really could make inferences might be hampered when they realized that B was not really a constant and reliable reference point. However, in view of our finding described in the last chapter (Lawrenson and Bryant, 1972) it seems unlikely that children can remember absolute sizes at all easily anyway, so this objection is probably not important. Moreover, the fact that this, and the rest of Smedslund's transitivity experiments, seem to support the developmental trend originally demonstrated by Piaget is certainly impressive. At first sight it does seem as though there are good reasons for believing with Piaget and Smedslund that young children do not make transitive inferences.

However, there are also good grounds for claiming that the traditional experiment has weaknesses in its design and these must be sorted out before one can reach any definite conclusions either way about the ability of young children to make inferences.

The design of the traditional transitivity experiment

No one disputes the discovery that young children generally fail and older children succeed with the traditional transitivity problems of the type administered by Piaget and by Smedslund. What is at stake is what these failures and successes mean. Two assumptions have been very widely made about the transitivity problem. The first is that the child who fails does not have the logical mechanism which is needed to co-ordinate separate items of information in an inference. The second is that a child who succeeds does possess this mechanism. It turns out that both assumptions can be criticized very severely.

We can take first the assumption about failures. The trouble with this assumption is that failures may well be caused by other factors than an inability to make inferences. An alternative possibility is that they could be due to lapses in memory. The transitivity problem is a successive one, and thus involves memory. When the child is finally asked the AC question he has to do at least two things. He must remember the AB and the BC comparisons, and he must put them together inferentially. It follows that failures could be due simply to the fact that the child does not remember the information, and that if he could remember it he could organize it in an inference perfectly well. Thus the meaning of failures in these tasks is ambiguous. They tell us nothing definite about logical ability.

The assumption about the meaning of successes is just as questionable. It is by no means certain that the child who answers the AC question correctly does so by making a genuine logical inference. He may produce the correct answer merely by parroting a verbal label picked up in the initial training. The point here is that the correct response to A in the initial AB comparison is 'larger', while to C in the initial BC comparison it is 'smaller'. Yet 'larger' is also the correct answer to A and 'smaller' to C, when the inferential comparison has to be made between A and C. So if the child simply remembers what he said about A or about C in the initial comparisons, he will give the right answer to the AC question for quite the wrong reasons. He certainly will not have made a genuine inference.

Both these difficulties have been noticed before (Smedslund, 1969). However, the traditional transitivity experiment does not control for them, and this means that its results are uninterpretable. Until quite recently it was impossible to find an experiment on transitive inferences which simultaneously ensured that failures were not the result of forgetting and that successes could not be written off as mere parroting.

Two basic precautions are needed to ensure that failures really are inferential failures and have nothing to do with forgetting. First the child should be given a lot of experience with the initial direct comparisons so that he will probably remember these comparisons later. Secondly, at the time when the child is asked the indirect inferential question he should also be tested for his memory of the initial comparisons on which the inference has to be based. Only if he can remember the initial comparisons, but cannot manage the inference, is it fair to conclude that his failure really is an inferential one.

The control against parroting is also fairly simple. All that is needed is to increase the number of quantities involved from three to five, where $A > B > C > D > E$. With five quantities one has four initial one-step comparisons, which are $A > B$, $B > C$, $C > D$, and $D > E$. Three of the five quantities, B, C and D, each occur in two of these comparisons and each is the smaller in one initial comparison and the larger in the other. This means that by the time the child is asked the inferential questions he will have seen B, C and D equally often as the smaller and the larger stimulus. Thus he will not be able to solve any inference which is based only on B, C and D by merely repeating a specific verbal label. There is only one inference which can be based just on these three values, and that is the inferential comparison between B and D. Any other new inferential comparison based on the four initial direct AB, BC, CD, and DE comparisons has to include either A or E or both, and since A is always the larger in this initial comparison and E always the smaller, these other inferences could be an unreliable test of a child's inferential ability.

The correct way to test for inferences in young children, therefore, is to have four initial direct comparisons, to make sure that the child knows these fairly thoroughly, to test the child's memory for them at the same time as testing his ability to combine them inferentially, and to make the BD question the crucial test of the child's ability to make inferences.

Alternative transitivity experiments

Some of these controls have been introduced by other experimenters, but none of their experiments has included all the controls in one study. For example, Braine (1959) in a well-known study with children between three and a half and seven years did make them very familiar with the material before posing the inferential problem. However, each of his problems involved only three quantities, and therefore the considerable successes obtained by the young children in this experiment could have been achieved without their ever having made an inference at all. Another study by Youniss and Murray (1970) with children of six and eight years did involve five quantities, and therefore tested genuine inferences. However, nothing was done in this study to control for memory failures. No steps were taken either to make the children reasonably familiar with the five quantities first or to check that they remembered the original direct comparison when they were asked the inferential question. Thus the consistent failures which Youniss and Murray found in their younger group could very well have been due to forgetting.

Because we could find no experiment which contained all the necessary controls, my colleague, Dr Tom Trabasso and I began a series of experiments in 1969 in order to find out as definitely as we possibly could whether young children can or cannot make deductive transitive inferences.

Our first experiment (Bryant and Trabasso, 1971) was with children of four, five, and six years, and was divided into two main stages, the first a training stage and the second a test stage. In the training stage it was ensured that the children got to know the four initial direct comparisons, $A > B$, $B > C$, $C > D$, and $D > E$. In the test stage we looked at two things, whether the child could remember these initial comparisons and whether he could combine them inferentially. In particular, the test stage was concerned with the children's answers to the BD question. Every child had to deal with five rods whose lengths and colours were different. Their lengths were $A = 7$ inches, $B = 6$ inches, $C = 5$ inches, $D = 4$ inches, and $E = 3$ inches. The colours were blue, red, green, yellow and white, and for each child a particular colour always signalled the same length, so that, for example, for one child A would always be blue, B green, C red and so on. We also used a black block of wood, which contained five holes and these holes had different depths. The five depths were 6 inches, 5 inches, 4 inches, 3 inches and 2 inches. The reason for having this block of wood was that it made it possible for us to show the child two rods of different lengths and yet protruding equally from the top of the block. Thus we could show the child two rods of different colours and ask him which was the longer without him being able to see which actually was the longer. This is a great help both for training the initial comparisons and for asking the inferential questions.

The training stage involved a series of trials in which the child had to make the four comparisons $A > B$, $B > C$, $C > D$ and $D > E$; but the trials were arranged in such a way that the child not only made the comparisons but also learned them. In each training trial one of the four pairs of rods was shown to the child, with the two rods side by side in the block of wood, both rods protruding by 1 inch. The child, who had no way of telling which was the longer simply by looking at them in this state, was then asked which of the two was the taller (or shorter). Once he had made his choice the two rods were taken out of the box and the child was shown, and told, which was the longer. Thus each training trial ended with the child being given visual and verbal feedback about the actual lengths of the two rods involved. This training continued until the child was able to choose correctly whenever he was shown a particular pair. The child first learned each of the four pairs separately and then was given them all again but in an intermingled manner, so that on one trial he would be asked about one pair, on the next about another and so on. This second training phase continued until the child consistently chose correctly whenever he was given any of the four pairs, until, in fact, he really knew that $A > B$, $B > C$, $C > D$ and $D > E$.

This training turned out to be surprisingly easy, though it sometimes took more than one session. Very few children even in the four-year-old group dropped out at this stage. Once the training had been completed they were moved on to the test stage. The same five rods and the same block of wood were used. Two things, however, were new. First, each child was asked about all ten possible comparisons (AB, BC, CD, DE, AC, AD, AE, *BD*, BE, CE). Notice that the first four of these are the initial comparisons, which means that the child's memory for these comparisons was being tested at this stage. The remaining six are all the possible new inferential comparisons that can be based on the four initial items. However, as has been mentioned, only one of these, the BD comparison, can be confidently regarded as genuinely inferential. Secondly, no feedback was ever given during the test phase. In each test trial a pair of rods, distinguishable as usual by their colour, was presented, again protruding 1 inch above the block of wood in which they were embedded. The child would be asked to say either which was the taller or which the shorter: but after he had made his choice he was never shown or told whether he was right or wrong. This was necessary because each of the ten pairs was presented four times during this stage, and the possibility that the child would, for example, get the BD pair right not through an inference, but simply by remembering the correct answer from the last BD trial, had to be eliminated.

This experiment produced some very consistent results, and these have since been repeated many times in many other versions of the same experimental design. All three age groups passed through the training stage fairly easily, though the older children learned the four compari-

sons faster than the younger ones. More important were the test
scores, which showed that children at all three age levels were very well
able to make transitive inferences. They remembered the initial comparisons fairly well, and they answered the crucial BD question correctly far more frequently than would be expected by chance. The per-
centage scores for all ten pairs are given in Table 3.1. This shows that
the four-year-olds were correct in 78 per cent of the BD trials, the
five-year-olds in 88 per cent and the six-year-olds in 92 per cent. So it

Table 3.1 Probability of correct choices on tests for transitivity and
retention (Experiment 1) (Bryant and Trabasso, 1971)

Stimulus	B	C	D	E
4-yr-old children				
A	0·96	0·96	0·93	0·98
B	—	0·92	0·78	0·92
C	—	—	0·90	0·94
D	—	—	—	0·91
5-yr-old children				
A	1·00	0·96	1·00	0·98
B	—	0·86	0·88	1·00
C	—	—	0·92	1·00
D	—	—	—	1·00
6-yr-old children				
A	0·99	0·99	1·00	1·00
B	—	0·94	0·92	0·99
C	—	—	0·98	1·00
D	—	—	—	1·00

seems that even children as young as four years can combine separate
perceptual experiences inferentially, provided that they can remember
the information which has to be combined. Moreover, their failure to
answer the BD question in a few of the trials was probably due not to
inferential errors, but to memory lapses. They did not recall the initial
BC and CD comparisons perfectly in the test stage which means that
they did not always remember the information on which the BD comparisons must be based. In fact, the BD errors made by all three age
groups can quite plausibly be accounted for in terms of the extent to
which they forgot the initial BC and CD comparisons (Bryant and
Trabasso, 1971).

This point about memory is interesting, but the most important thing about these results is that the children's correct answers to the BD question were always significantly greater than would be expected by chance. This is strong evidence that young children can make transitive inferences very well, and therefore that Piaget's and Smedslund's hypothesis about children and inferences is far too pessimistic. There is, however, still one possible objection to concluding finally from this experiment that children can make inferences, and this concerns the possibility that they remembered the absolute lengths of B and of D. The children actually saw the full lengths of each rod at the end of every training trial, and by remembering the actual lengths they could work out that B was longer than D without having to connect B and D through their common relations with C.

It is very unlikely, in view of the great difficulty children have in remembering absolute sizes, that this is a serious objection. However, their difficulty with absolute values has not been specifically demonstrated with rods of the sort used and so the possibility that absolute memory had affected the results of our experiment could not be ruled out. We, therefore, designed another experiment to find out whether young children can make inferences even when they cannot know the absolute lengths of the rods involved.

There are various ways of eliminating absolute cues. We did it simply by cutting out the visual feedback during the training phase. In this second experiment (Bryant and Trabasso, 1971) which involved four- and five-year-old children, the procedure was identical to that of the first experiment except for one detail. At the end of each training trial, after the child had made his choice, he was only told whether he was right or wrong. He was never shown the whole length of any of the rods, and thus only saw them sticking out an inch from the top of the black block. He was, therefore, unable to learn the absolute length of the rods.

This generally made the training phase longer and more difficult, but otherwise the results were as clear cut as in the first experiment. They are presented in Table 3.2. The four-year-olds' answers to the BD question were correct 82 per cent of the time and the five-year-olds' 85 per cent. Again their few failures in the BD comparisons could be accounted for by the fact that their memory for the BC and CD initial comparisons was not perfect. This experiment demonstrates conclusively that young children are capable of making genuine transitive inferences.

Table 3.2 Probability of correct choices on tests for transitivity and retention (Experiment 2) (Bryant and Trabasso, 1971)

Stimulus	B	C	D	E
4-yr-old children				
A	0·98	0·98	0·93	0·97
B	—	0·89	0·82	0·90
C	—	—	0·87	0·88
D	—	—	—	0·94
5-yr-old children				
A	0·98	0·92	0·95	0·97
B	—	0·87	0·85	0·98
C	—	—	0·97	0·95
D	—	—	—	0·98

Two main points follow from this conclusion. The first is that Piaget's theory about logical development must, to some extent, be wrong. His experiments did not ensure that children could remember the comparisons which they were asked to combine inferentially, and it now seems clear that children can manage this sort of inference provided that they can remember the information on which the inference has to be based. The second point is that this evidence shows that children have the logical mechanism for using framework cues as a basis for organizing and categorizing their perceptual experience through perceptual inferences.

However, as well as showing that children can make transitive inferences, these experiments also seem to show that what the child remembers may be an important factor in determining whether or not he is going to make an inference successfully. It therefore becomes important to examine the exact relationship between the child's memory for perceptual comparisons and his ability to combine them in an inference.

Inference and memory

The two experiments, which have just been described, show that young children who do remember relative judgements can combine them inferentially. The experiments do not, however, demonstrate that the child's inferences are entirely dependent on memory. It is not possible, for example, to claim that as soon as a child had grasped and could remember the fact that B > C and that C > D, he could immediately make the BD inference, because the training phase lasted some time and was kept rigidly separate from the test phase. There could have been some time during the training phase when the child had learnt and remembered that B > C and C > D, and yet was still not able to combine these two direct comparisons in an inference. Our experiments were not sufficiently sensitive to rule out this possibility of a temporary period during which the child could remember two items but could not co-ordinate them, and one cannot conclude from them that memory is a sufficient as well as a necessary condition for inferences in young children.

Another experiment was needed, therefore, to monitor the child's memory for the initial comparisons and at the same time his ability to combine them inferentially, trial by trial, right through the experiment. Suppose, for example, that the child goes through a series of trials, in each of which he is first given the basic information about the four direct comparisons A > B, B > C, C > D and D > E, and then is immediately tested both for his ability to remember these four comparisons and also for his ability to make the BD inference. Once this presentation-test sequence is finished in one trial, the next trial begins, where the same sequence is repeated, and then the next trial and so on. Thus trial by trial we can measure how well the child is grasping the four direct comparisons, and at the same time how successfully he is managing to make the BD inference. This procedure (which people who are familiar with experiments on verbal learning will recognize as very similar to paired associate learning) will show whether the child makes the inference as soon as he can remember the relevant initial comparisons, BC and CD, or whether there has to be an intervening period when he has the necessary information but cannot use it inferentially.

This trial-by-trial task is quite a difficult one for young children. We found (Bryant, 1973) that the easiest way to present the problem was not to use coloured rods, but to tell the child stories about how we visited a house where we met some children, and how we met different pairs of children at different times and noticed that in each case one of the two was taller than the other, that Jane, A, was taller than Tom, B, that Tom was taller than Susan, C, and so on. Having heard this story once, the child is immediately tested to see if he remembers the four pairs, and also whether he can make the BD inference. Thus in the presentation stage of each trial the child is told once about four comparisons AB, BC, CD and DE and in the test stage he is asked five questions, four of them about the initial comparisons and the fifth about the BD inference. He is never told whether his answer to these questions is right or wrong. This procedure constitutes one trial and when it is completed another similar trial begins. The whole procedure lasts until the child is consistently correct with all five questions in the test stage.

We tried this task out with five-year-old children, and the results showed very clearly that they had only to remember the BC and CD comparisons to be able to make an inference. As soon as they began to answer the BC and the CD questions correctly, they also began to be consistently right about the BD inference. The only trouble with this experiment was that quite a few of the children never managed to be consistently correct about any of the comparisons direct or indirect. There is no doubt that the task is a particularly difficult one for young children. Nevertheless, the majority of them did eventually remember the initial comparisons, and without exception these children all also made the BD inference at the same time.

This last experiment demonstrates a clear relationship between the inferences which a child can make and the information which he can remember. The fact that children can apparently co-ordinate information they can remember does strongly suggest that when errors do occur in inference problems, these errors are most probably the result of memory failures. At any rate we can now finally reject the evidence of the traditional transitivity experiment which does not control for failures in memory. It is clear that young children can combine relative judgements which they do remember. They can make inferences.

Learning theory and deductive inferences

Piaget and Smedslund are not the only psychologists who have tried to show that young children cannot make inferences. A very different theoretical background has also produced much the same hypothesis. Over the last fifteen years or so Kendler and Kendler (1967), whose background is that of S–R learning theory, have also maintained that children younger than approximately eight years of age cannot make deductive inferences.

The inference problem tackled by the Kendlers has nothing to do with relative judgements, and to that extent their work is less relevant to the central argument of this book than are, for example, the experiments of Piaget and Smedslund. Nevertheless, they have consistently argued that young children cannot combine separate experiences.

The Kendlers derived their original ideas about children's inferences from experimental work on inferences in rats. Their starting point was a series of rat experiments carried out by Maier (1939) which appeared to show that rats can to some extent combine separate and different learned routines in order to solve a problem inferentially. The Kendlers' aim was to see if young children could do any better, and they designed a series of tasks in which a child was taught two components of a problem separately and was then tested to see if he could put the two together to solve the problem.

There were some specific differences of method between their early work (1956) and their later studies (1961). However, all the experiments followed the same general pattern. In one typical experiment five-year-old and eight-year-old children and also college students were set in front of an apparatus which contained three panels side by side. There was a button in the middle of the two side panels and an open tray at the bottom of each panel. There was also a circular opening in the middle and an open tray at the bottom of the centre panel.

Initially, the child had to learn two separate things. One of these was that pressing the button on one side panel produced a marble in that panel's tray, while pressing the other panel's button produced a ball bearing. The experimenters first showed the child that one button produced the marble, the other the ball bearing, and then over a series of trials gave him sometimes a marble and sometimes a ball bearing, asking him each time to press the button which produced the thing 'like this'. The other item which the child had to learn was that dropping one of these objects (the marble for half the children, the ball bearing for the other half) into the opening in the central panel produced a reward, which was a small charm. To teach the child this the experimenters gave him both objects over a series of trials, and asked him each time to insert the correct object, that is to say, the object which produced the charm.

When the child had mastered both these items, he was simply given the three panels and told to get himself the charm. The question was whether he would be able to combine the two items, which he had already learned, by first pressing the button which produced the 'correct' object and then putting it into the hole in the central panel.

The important thing about the results of the Kendlers' experiment was that the performance of the younger children was abysmal. Many of the five-year-olds did nothing, and those who did do something responded in a haphazard manner. Even the performance of the eight-year-olds was barely above chance level, and the only people to respond with consistent success were the college students. The Kendlers concluded that young children, like rats, cannot on the whole co-ordinate separate experiences, and their explanation of this failure was that each experience involves a different response, and thus on an S–R basis has to be treated quite separately from the other.

This is a somewhat depressing conclusion and it can be questioned for two main reasons. One is that we have already seen that children can combine two judgements inferentially, and that they can do so even though they respond to the common element differently in the two judgements. For example, when they combine the information that $A > B$ and that $B > C$ to infer that $A > C$ their response to B is 'smaller' in one judgement and 'larger' in the other, and yet they clearly connect A and C through the common element, B. So, if the children cannot in the Kendlers' experiment combine different experiences their failure may have something specifically to do with the details of the actual task. Indeed, the second worry about the Kendlers' experiment is the rather artificial nature of their task. Pressing buttons to produce marbles, and putting marbles into holes to obtain a charm are not everyday experiences for a young child, and it may be that he is so bemused by the oddness of the situation that he fails to exercise his normal ability to put different experiences together in an effectively logical manner.

There is one very striking piece of evidence which supports this second criticism, albeit somewhat obliquely, since the evidence involves not a developmental but a cross-cultural experiment. Cole, Gay, Glick and Sharp (1971) repeated the Kendler study just described with three groups of non-literate Liberians whose ages were five to six years, nine to twelve years, and seventeen to nineteen years. All three groups produced conspicuously poor performances and the two older groups were vastly inferior to 'literate' control groups. However, the experimenters did not conclude that these non-literate people were unable to make inferences. They had been impressed by the fact that many of the uneducated people in the experiment had shown signs of fear or of reticence, tending in the final stage of the experiment to wait around and to do nothing, apparently looking for further instructions. Cole *et al.* concluded that the strangeness of their apparatus might have been so daunting to these people that they were reduced to an essentially passive state. 'Up to this point' their report runs 'our work provides a model of how not to do a cross-cultural experiment because we really have no way to decide among various explanations for our findings. Is it fear of the electric apparatus that makes our subjects slow to respond, or are the instructions unclear? Or is it some difficulty in making arbitrary, although seemingly simple inferences of the sort this experiment tries to elicit?'

So they designed another experiment with the same general scheme but with more familiar material. The people in this experiment were presented with two easily distinguished matchboxes, and learned that one box contained a black key, and the other a red one. They were then told that one of the two keys would open a lock of a box which contained a piece of candy which they could eat when they found it. When they had learned which was the correct key they were given the whole problem again, and the question again was whether they could combine the two separate segments of the task. The non-literate people in this second experiment were all adults and thus it is quite reasonable to compare their performance with that of the oldest non-literate group in the first experiment. The performance of the non-literate adults was well above chance in this new version of the inference task and they were therefore much better than the equivalent non-literate group in the first experiment which used the Kendlers' equipment. It seems that non-literate Liberians are able to combine separate experiences, and only fail in the rather artificial Kendler situation through some specific experimental detail which has nothing to do with inferences.

The reservations expressed by Cole et al. were about the reactions of Africans with little education in experimental gadgetry. However, there is no reason why these reservations should not also apply to the five-year-old Western child. Why should he not also find the equipment and the arbitrary sequence of events strange and even frightening? Some recent and unpublished work done in Oxford (Hewson, unpublished material) has shown that children as young as three years old are able to combine the separate segments of a task very like the Kendlers', provided that different material is used. For example, if instead of pressing a button the child has to open a drawer to obtain a particular reward his performance in the final inferential stage is much better.

It is, then, plausible to suggest that young children can put two learned routines together, and that their failure in the Kendlers' task is not an inferential failure. In fact, the conclusions which we have reached about the Kendlers' experimental problem and about the traditional transitivity problem are much the same. Both apparently demonstrate that young children cannot make inferences, and yet it emerges that the failures which young children typically make in both problems probably tell us nothing about their inferential ability.

One lesson to be learned from this kind of analysis is how risky it is to conclude that some ability definitely does not exist in children. One is reminded of the child who kept on meeting the man who wasn't there and wishing that he would go away. Abilities which have been definitively ruled out in young children by one psychologist have a habit of cropping up in the experiments of another. It is, on the whole, much safer to say that something is difficult than that it is impossible.

Passive versus active inference problems

The inference problems which I have described so far are essentially passive problems, in that the child is always given all the essential information on which the inference must be based. This information is handed to him on a plate. He is told, for example, that $A > B$ and that $B > C$, before being asked the AC question, and he does not have to set about actively gathering the necessary information for himself.

Suppose, however, that the task is turned around. The child is told first that he has to find out about how A and C compare, even though he is not allowed to compare them directly, and he is shown that B is available and is a possible means of making a connexion between A and C. In this case, the child has to gather the information by himself by spontaneously using B as a ruler which will show him that $A > B$ and $B > C$. This way round the inference problem is an active rather than a passive one. The child has not only to make the inference, but also to get hold of the information on which the inference must be based. It would certainly be very interesting to know how children cope with an active version of the inference problem.

We have actually had information for some time about children's reactions to a task which involves active inferences. Again we owe the information to Piaget and his colleagues. In the best known of Piaget's active, or in his terms, 'spontaneous', inference problems (Piaget, Inhelder, and Szeminska, 1960; Piaget, 1953) he first showed children aged between five and nine years a tower of bricks piled on top of a small table and then asked them to build on another table another tower as tall as the first one. The two table tops were actually of different heights, and the children's task was not to line up the tops of the two towers, but to make sure that their absolute lengths were the same. A rod which was the same length as the first tower was left lying around. The point of this set-up was that the child could not compare the two towers directly because they started from bases of different heights. (One can notice incidentally again that a child with an effective absolute code for length would be able to make this comparison without the help of an inference. Piaget's covert assumption is in line with my argument that young children find it difficult to respond on the basis of absolute sizes.) So the child needed some intervening common reference point, which could be taken and compared directly to both towers and through which the two could be connected. The solution is to take the rod, B, to the first tower, A, and having found that their lengths are the same to build another tower, C, to the height of B.

In fact, the five-year-old children did not use the rod as a measure. Piaget does report that some six-year-olds tended to use their bodies as a way of comparing the two towers, and this on the whole proved a rather inefficient form of measurement. When, for example, a child put one hand at the bottom and the other at the top of one of the towers and then went over to the second tower trying to keep his hands a constant distance apart, he was almost certain to make an inaccurate comparison. Nevertheless, despite the slapstick element there is obviously evidence here of some idea of an intervening measure. From the age of seven years onwards the children began to use the rod spontaneously as a way of comparing the two towers, and thus showed quite clearly both that they could understand that $A = C$ where $A = B$ and $B = C$, and also that they knew how to gather the information needed to make such an inference.

The most important result here is the complete failure of children younger than six years to use the inference principle 'spontaneously'. Piaget himself sees this as yet another clear indication that young children cannot make inferences. However, we have already found that they can make inferences in a passive situation where they are given the information which they then have to combine. It is possible, therefore, that there is an important difference between passive and active problems, and that young children can manage in a passive situation but not in an active one.

One can quibble at Piaget's experiment which is certainly not entirely convincing. The instructions given to the children might have been unclear, and they might not, for example, have understood that the experimenter was referring to the height from the table tops and not from the floor. However, we have evidence (Bryant, 1973) which supports Piaget's contention that young children have great difficulties with active inference problems. We found that children who had actually done extremely well in our passive inference problems were quite incapable of solving an active version of this task in which they had to get hold of the right information before they made the inference. Here, then, were children who could make an inference, but who could not put their inferential ability to use in an active situation.

It would seem that there may well be a gap between potential and performance, between what a child can do and what he eventually does do. He can make inferences, but is not very good at creating a situation in which inferences can be made. This does not mean that he will never make inferences in real life, because there will be situations which are essentially passive and in which all the necessary information is provided. However, it does seem that there will be situations in which the young child will not be able to bring his inferential ability into play.

No doubt this gap diminishes with age, and it is quite possible that it does so largely as a result of the child's experiences when he is taught how to measure at school. Indeed, it may be that the aspect of the question of children's inferences which is most relevant to education is this difference between passive and active inferences.

My conclusions suggest that when the child is initially being taught to measure, he needs to be told not how to make inferences but how to make his inferential ability most effective. He needs to be taught not that $A > C$ when $A > B$ and $B > C$, but how to use B as a ruler. Of course, measurement involves a great many more manoeuvres than this: and my comments apply only to the very beginnings of measurement. Nonetheless, the discovery that children can make transitive inferences provided that the situation is right may make the apparently formidable task of teaching a child how to measure seem a little less daunting.

Perceptual inferences

The evidence presented in this chapter suggests that young children can make inferences very well indeed even though they may have some difficulty in gathering the information on which inferences can be based. Although this conclusion is obviously relevant to theories about logical development such as Piaget's, only its implications for the subject of perceptual development will be pursued here. There are two main implications, one of which concerns young children's use of perceptual frameworks, the other the relationship of perceptual to cognitive development.

The first point is that the demonstration that children can make transitive inferences means that they do have the logical basis for using frameworks when they make perceptual judgements and for basing these judgements on perceptual inferences. If a child can work out that A = C whenever A = B and B = C, he has the basis for realizing, for example, that two objects which he sees at quite different times but which are both parallel to a particular framework feature are in the same orientation. To use Piaget's example, he has the basis for working out that the level of liquid tends to stay the same by noticing that it is constantly parallel to a horizontal framework feature. Of course, to demonstrate that children can make inferences does not mean that they necessarily use these inferences when they make perceptual judgements. It only establishes that they have the logical basis to do so.

The second point concerns the passive-active inference distinction. The point is that the perceptual inferences in my hypothesis belong to the passive and not at all to the active category. If a child is given direct comparisons then, provided that he can remember them, he manages inferences well. If he has to seek out a measure, detach it from its surroundings and apply it before he makes an inference, then he is usually at a loss.

In the perceptual inferences which I have been describing the intervening measure is the background, the constant external framework. The child compares different objects which he sees at different times through their common relations to a constant background. This background is given. The child does not have to fetch it and apply it to A and to C. So the child who can manage a passive inference problem certainly ought in principle to be able to make the kind of inference which I am suggesting may be a basic feature of the perceptual judgements made by young children. Now that we have established that young children can manage passive inferences, we can go on to ask whether they rely on these inferences in perceptual situations.

4
Orientation

Thus far we have established two things. The first is that the young child has a need to make perceptual inferences in order to compare objects which he sees at different times. The second is that he has the logical ability to make such inferences, which would have to be deductive ones. The next step is to see whether he really does rely on perceptual inferences when he handles information from perceptual continua.

This chapter will deal with perceptual inferences which the child makes about orientation. It may seem a little odd to start with orientation when the last two chapters have dealt mainly with the way children handle size differences. However, it is with orientation that we have the clearest evidence that the young child relies on perceptual inferences, and that his dependence on these inferences diminishes as he grows older.

Different objects are seen in particular orientations and the same object appears in different orientations on different occasions. These different orientations can be coded both relatively and absolutely. A relative code would tell you about the similarities and differences between objects. On the other hand an absolute code would tell you, for example, whether a particular line were vertical or horizontal or a 45° oblique.

My argument will simply be that young children initially adopt relative codes for orientation. They remember orientations primarily through their relationships to features of the background. As they grow older, they rely less and less on these background relationships because they begin to acquire the internal categories for particular orientations which form the basis for an absolute code.

This hypothesis is very simple and takes a form which by now will be very familiar to the reader. However, the area itself is rather complex.

Many other psychologists have been interested in how young children handle information about orientation and have approached the problem in many different ways. Some, for example, have been mainly interested in the question of attention to orientation, and others in the difficulty children have in distinguishing mirror-images and the relationship of this difficulty to the symmetry of the central nervous system. These different approaches have produced a heterogeneous set of data. It is, I think, quite possible to account for this variety of data with one hypothesis, but inevitably the argument becomes complex.

Attentional theory and the child's ability to solve simultaneous discriminations

Some of the most striking evidence about the way children compare and discriminate orientation has been provoked by the well-known attentional theory put forward by E. J. Gibson. This theory, which is very well described in her recent book (Gibson, 1969), is quite complex in that it covers very many aspects of perceptual development. However, its basic principle is quite simple. Gibson argues that children and adults can only take in a limited amount of information at any one time and therefore attend only to some aspects of what is going on around them and not to others. Gibson's view is that we select what to attend to in a systematic way. She argues that children and adults tend to attend to particular dimensions or distinctive features and not to others, so that, for example, they may take in information about the size of objects around them but ignore their colour. Moreover, they choose which dimension to ignore and which to attend to in an extremely rational manner. They attend to categories of information which their past experience has shown them are relevant to their behaviour, and they reject information which they have learned to be irrelevant.

This is a theory about development because Gibson's very interesting argument is that the relevance of particular dimensions changes with age. A dimension which is quite irrelevant to the things which a three-year-old does might be highly significant for the sort of acts which a five-year-old wants to perform. Gibson argues that this will mean that children may attend to different things at different ages. The older child may learn that a category of information or dimension which he had regarded as useless has suddenly become important, and will begin to take in information which when he was younger he ignored altogether.

In fact, Gibson's clearest example of this kind of developmental change is the child's perception of orientation. She argues that the orientation of an object is irrelevant to the pre-school child because the orientation of the objects he encounters will tend to vary from occasion to occasion. The child will see a toy, for example, sometimes standing up, sometimes on its back and sometimes upside down. Remembering the toy's orientation is not going to help the child recognize it on another occasion.

However, when the child goes to school he has to learn to read and orientation, at any rate of letters, becomes very important to him. If he does not take in information about orientation he will not learn to distinguish, for example, between b and d. Therefore, Gibson argues, the young pre-school child is generally unaware of orientation differences, while the older child who has begun to learn to read starts attending to this type of information.

Gibson and her colleagues have produced an impressive volume of data to show that young children are very much worse than older children at handling information about orientation. However, many of their experiments are very difficult to interpret because they concern learning tasks, which naturally involve not only perceptual experiences but also memory. Discrimination learning experiments will tell us nothing definite about a child's attention to orientation, because if we talk about attention we are really concerned with what the child is aware of in his immediate experience and not with what he can remember.

There is however one important and very well known experiment devised by Gibson and her colleagues (Gibson, Gibson, Pick and Osser, 1962) which avoids these ambiguities by using a simultaneous matching problem. They gave children of four to eight years a matching task consisting of several trials, and in each trial the children were shown one standard shape on the top of the display and below this several other shapes. At least one of these latter shapes was identical to the standard, while most differed from the standard along one dimension or another. One of these dimensions was orientation (described as 'rotation and reversal'), so that there was always at least one card on which the figure was exactly the same as the standard except for the fact that it was in another orientation. Another was the so-called break–close dimension: the child was shown a shape like the standard except for some breaks in the lines.

The child's task in each trial was to select the choice cards exactly like the standard and reject the rest. The results of the experiment were very striking. The younger the children were, the more orientation errors they made. By the age of about eight years they made very few. This developmental difference was specific because the number of errors on other dimensions, such as the break–close dimension, did not change much with age. Thus it seems that the orientation errors cannot simply be explained in terms of children getting generally better at matching tasks. So the experimenters concluded that it is between the ages of four and eight years that the child learns to attend to orientation, a dimension he initially ignores but later finds to be important. Since at four years he has not yet gone to school while at eight years he is at school and has had considerable experience of being taught to read, Gibson and her colleagues argue that it may be because eight-year-olds have learned that orientation differences can be quite important that they attend to these differences.

At first sight this is a very plausible explanation for these interesting results. However, there are perhaps at least two good reasons for rejecting the Gibson hypothesis, at least in its present form. One is that the hypothesis itself is a very odd one. It is absolutely true as Gibson claims that remembering a toy's orientation will not help the child much when he has to recognize the toy on another occasion. This, however, is a question of memory, not of perception. There are, on the other hand, very good reasons for thinking that orientation information is extremely important to the immediate perceptually-guided behaviour even of very young children. Take the example of a young child placing one brick on top of another, a skill which he possesses a very long time indeed before he goes to school. This quite clearly is something which must depend on perceiving the orientation of the bricks. Here then is one example out of a whole range of perceptuo-motor activities which are in the young child's repertoire and which must depend on his being able to attend to the way in which objects around him are oriented.

The second worry about Gibson's analysis concerns experimental method. The experiment is by far the most direct evidence offered for the attentional approach to children's perception of orientation. It involves a simultaneous matching problem rather than a discrimination task. However, even here we can question whether it really is a test of attention. The trouble is that although it is a simultaneous matching experiment the actual display used is far too complex, involving several dozen choice cards. When a child has to look through so many choices he probably no longer makes a direct comparison between each choice figure and the standard, but instead commits the standard to memory before he begins to search through the choices. Thus this experiment, too, may be about memory. There is in fact some very good evidence that young children of four and five years can attend to information about orientation and can use it very effectively when they are given comparisons which are genuinely simultaneous. When the display involves far fewer choice stimuli than Gibson's, young children do seem to respond to orientation differences very consistently.

The simplest possible orientation matching task is a two-choice problem in which the child is shown three figures side by side and has to say, for example, which of the two outside ones is identical to the figure in the middle. There are at least three experiments which show that four- and five-year-old children can solve a simultaneous two-choice task of this kind. This ability was originally demonstrated by Over and Over (1967) in a matching task in which children as young as four years were shown three straight lines simultaneously and were asked which of the two choice lines was in the same orientation as the standard line. They made remarkably few errors. Some later experiments of my own (Bryant 1969, 1973) have amply confirmed that five-year-old children can solve simultaneous, two-choice matching problems very easily when the stimuli are three straight lines which differ only in orientation.

So it seems that young children can attend to orientation when the display is a simple one, and this result certainly supports the suggestion that the orientation errors found by Gibson and her colleagues were errors of memory rather than genuinely attentional ones. Moreover, some other results in the Overs' experiments and in my own support this further. The experiments also included successive problems in which children were first shown the standard on its own. This was then removed and after a set interval they were shown two choice lines and asked to point out the one whose orientation was the same as the standard. Thus the experiments compared matches which involved memory with matches which did not, and what emerged was that young children had difficulties in the successive rather than in the simultaneous tasks. Actually, the difficulties which did occur in the successive comparisons were rather specific: they occurred in some successive comparisons and not in others. This specific pattern will be described in detail in the next section. At this stage we can simply note that children can apparently cope with simultaneous comparisons very efficiently, and only make an appreciable number of errors when they have to remember orientation.

So all the objections to the attentional hypothesis point to the same conclusion, that children notice orientation in the immediate perceptual situation, and that their main problems are with *remembering* orientations. This conclusion fits in very well with a relative analysis of orientation. If the child can detect whether lines parallel each other or not without taking in their actual orientations, he is using a relative and not an absolute code.

Of course, there is still the alternative possibility that children use an absolute code for orientation, and simply forget the orientations of the figures which they have seen. This would also lead to good performance in simultaneous tasks and poor performance in successive ones. However, the next section will show that the very specific errors which young children produce in successive tasks make this absolute analysis most implausible. At any rate, we can conclude for the moment that young children do attend to information about orientation and that a successful hypothesis must explain why they have difficulties with some successive comparisons.

Discriminations between obliques and the question of symmetry

We have known for some time that young children's difficulties with successive orientation comparisons are very specific. Some are very easy, and others extremely hard. The best contrast involves discriminations between two oblique lines pointing in opposite directions and between a horizontal and a vertical line. The first of these is very difficult, the second rather easy for young children. A pattern as specific as this is very valuable to the experimental psychologist because it might offer a direct clue to the underlying perceptual mechanisms involved. But this particular pattern of behaviour becomes even more interesting when one realizes that it occurs in many animal species as well. The most direct evidence for the difference between oblique–oblique and horizontal–vertical discriminations comes from discrimination learning experiments with a wide range of species; in fact the original comparison was made in experiments with animals of one sort and another. Lashley (1938) originally found that rats learn a horizontal–vertical discrimination more easily than one between obliques. Sutherland (1957) repeated this observation with octopuses and Mackintosh and Sutherland (1963) with goldfish. A pattern of behaviour as specific and widespread as this is bound to catch the attention of comparative psychologists, and it is not at all surprising that an attempt was soon made to see whether something similar occurs in young children as well.

The first systematic evidence about young children's ability to learn discriminations between obliques and between horizontal and vertical lines came from a now well-known experiment which Rudel and Teuber (1963) carried out with children aged between three and a half and eight and a half years. This was a complex experiment in which each child was given a series of discrimination tasks. In one of these he was shown on every trial two square plaques, one of which had a horizontal line, the other a vertical line across it. In another task the two plaques showed oblique lines, pointing in different directions. The children were told in each task that one of the cards was right, the other wrong, and that they had to learn which was the right one.

This experiment produced a most interesting contrast between age groups. There were virtually no differences between them in the horizontal–vertical tasks. However, the younger children made many more errors than the older ones when the discrimination was between two obliques. Thus we now have two main points to consider: first, oblique–oblique discriminations appear to be particularly difficult; secondly, this specific difficulty diminishes as the child grows older. These are important conclusions, but at this stage they can only be regarded as very preliminary, because the evidence leaves two important questions totally unanswered.

The first concerns the distinction between perception and memory, a question which comes up time and again in the study of the perception of orientation. The second is about the influence of symmetry. The first arises simply because all the experiments described were discrimination experiments. The second concerns a very interesting topic, which will feature largely in this chapter and the next: mirror-images. In all the experiments just described the lines in the oblique pairs were presented side by side and were symmetrical around the vertical axis. (Figures symmetrical around the vertical or horizontal axis are usually described as mirror-images.) Are the obliques difficult because they are mirror-images? The question is still very much open because all the experiments described so far used only symmetrical pairs of obliques, and did not introduce non mirror-image pairs.

Obliques and the perception/memory question

It was Over and Over (1967) who first pointed out that the orientation discrimination experiments did not allow one to sort out whether errors were due to failures in perception or in memory, and who originally showed that the relative difficulty with obliques simply does not occur in simultaneous matching tasks. My experiments with four- and five-year-olds (Bryant 1969, 1973) which I shall describe in more detail in the next section, have also confirmed this.

Two points can be made about the results of these later matching experiments. First, the young child can tell obliques apart as easily as he can horizontals and verticals. Secondly, the discovery of the specific effect in successive comparisons may mean that the question of memory failures is also rather specific. If children have difficulty in remembering orientation, they apparently have difficulty with some orientations very much more than with others. Later I shall try to show that these specific memory lapses can be explained in terms of the perceptual inferences which the typical framework does and does not allow the child to make.

Symmetry

Many people have thought that young children are particularly prone to confuse figures which are mirror-images of each other. One of the first suggestions that young children are especially confused by these was made by Ernst Mach in his book *The Analysis of Sensations* (1959), which was originally published in 1893. Mach was impressed by the fact that the body and particularly the visual system is symmetrical around the vertical axis, and he argued that this may lead to confusions between figures which are symmetrical in the same way. He writes, 'Without entering into particulars we may observe first that the whole apparatus of the eye and especially the motor apparatus is symmetrical with respect to the median plane of the head. Hence symmetrical movements of looking will be connected with like or approximately like space sensations. Children constantly confound the letters b and d, p and q. Adults, too, do not readily notice a change from left to right, unless some special points of apprehension for sense or intellect make it noticeable.' Mach also notes that the whole body is 'affected with a slight asymmetry' which leads one to prefer, for example, to use the right hand rather than the left. He suggests that this asymmetry, which is stronger and more consistent in adults than in children, provides the basic cue for telling apart left from right and thus for distinguishing mirror-image figures which are symmetrical around the vertical axis. Thus in Mach's opinion both our original difficulties with mirror-images and our eventual success in being able to tell them apart are directly linked to our physical make-up.

A very similar analysis was produced by Orton (1937) some years later. Orton's main interest was in the symmetry of the two halves of the nervous system and particularly in the fact that the two cerebral hemispheres are more or less exact mirror-images of each other. His main thesis was that seeing a figure involves exactly the same pattern of firing in the two hemispheres except that the pattern in the left hemisphere is the mirror-image of that in the right. He suggested that this meant that children would be likely to confuse left-right mirror-image pairs because the two figures would produce exactly that same pattern of excitation, though reversed between hemispheres. Orton also argued that children eventually overcome this confusion when these two hemispheres take on different and specialized functions, and in particular when the so-called 'dominant hemisphere' begins to control the child's speech. Like Mach, Orton argues that the child only has a basis for telling symmetrical figures apart when he has developed some internal asymmetry of his own.

Mach and Orton were concerned mainly with confusions between letters and words, but their ideas are also directly relevant to obliques. Certainly, experimenters seem to think that the difficulty with obliques is something directly to do with their being mirror-images. Moreover, there has been at least one recent and notable attempt to argue for the idea that the special difficulties associated with left-right mirror images, particularly obliques, may have something to do with the organization of the central nervous system (Corballis and Beale, 1970, 1971).

Two comments ought to be made about this analysis. The first is simply that whatever the confusions are they are not straightforward perceptual confusions, since young children discriminate simultaneously presented mirror-image obliques very well. It is very difficult to see how Orton's hypothesis could deal with this fact. The second is that the experiments described did not establish that the difficulty with obliques really is a mirror-image one, since they only used pairs which were symmetrical around the vertical axis. None introduced asymmetrical pairs as a control. Children may confuse *any* pair, mirror-image or not. Of course, it could be argued that any oblique pair is still a mirror-image around some axis which is itself oblique. But that line of argument would also have to describe the easy horizontal–vertical pairs as mirror-images. Only an analysis restricted to symmetry around the vertical (and perhaps the horizontal) axis can explain the evidence. As I have shown the proper test of this mirror-image analysis is to introduce pairs of obliques which are not, in the conventional use of the phrase, mirror-images.

There are two experiments with young children which have introduced this control (Bryant, 1969, 1972) and both show fairly clearly that the difficulty which young children have with obliques has little or nothing to do with the question of symmetry and mirror-images.

The first of these (Bryant, 1969, Exp. 2) was with five-year-old children who were given just a series of successive two-choice matching problems. In each trial they were shown first a standard line on its own. This line was then removed and after an interval of five seconds they were shown two more lines in different orientations. One choice was identical to the standard, the other's orientation was different. Each child was given three types of comparison. In one the two choice lines were *mirror-image obliques*. Throughout the experiment the obliques used were either 22·5 degrees or 67·5 degrees off vertical, and this meant that in the mirror-image comparisons the two choice obliques were either both 22·5 degrees or both 67·5 degrees off vertical. The second type of comparison was also between two obliques but this time between *non mirror-image obliques*. If the standard and the correct choice lines were 22·5 degrees off vertical, the incorrect choice which pointed in the opposite direction was always 67·5 degrees off vertical, and vice versa. The third kind of comparison was between an oblique and either a horizontal or a vertical line with the oblique as standard. On any analysis this last comparison should be easy, since there is no question of symmetry, and horizontal or vertical lines are involved. This comparison was put in as a control to check that the children understood what the the successive matching task involved.

The results were very clear. They are shown in Table 4.1. Both types of oblique–oblique comparison, mirror- and non mirror-image, were extremely difficult. Scores on both hovered around chance level. On the other hand, the successive comparison between obliques and horizontals or verticals proved extremely easy. Thus the children understood what they had to do, but nevertheless were unable to distinguish between successively presented obliques, symmetrical or not.

Table 4.1 Mean correct choices out of 10 in first mirror-image experiment (Bryant, 1969)

Standard	Choice	Simultaneous group		Successive group	
		Mean	S.D.	Mean	S.D.
O	O vs O (mirror images)	8·73	1·24	5·93	1·84
O	O vs O (non-mirror images)	8·87	1·36	5·53	2·25
O	O vs H or V	9·07	0·93	8·47	1·12

O = Oblique; H = horizontal; V = vertical.

Obviously it would be very difficult for a mirror-image analysis to handle these results. However, it could be argued that the experiment was a very restricted one, since it dealt only with five-year-olds, used only two oblique orientations and involved only successive comparisons. The next experiment (Bryant, 1973, Exp. 1) confirms and extends the conclusion that the difficulty associated with obliques does not in any way depend on symmetry.

In this experiment we saw children of four, five, six and seven years, giving half of them simultaneous comparisons with all three lines present at the same time, and the other half successive comparisons with a five-second delay between the presentation of the standard and the two choice lines. Each child was faced with four types of comparison: between (1) mirror-image obliques (2) non mirror-image obliques (3) an oblique and either a horizontal or a vertical, with the oblique as the standard, and (4) either a horizontal or a vertical and an oblique, with the horizontal or vertical as standard.

We used a greater variety of slopes with our obliques this time. Every child at different times saw obliques whose angles were 15, 30, 45, 60 and 75 degrees off vertical. In the mirror-image comparisons the two obliques pointed in opposite directions but had the same slope. In the non mirror-image comparisons, on the other hand, the two obliques always had different slopes and each slope was systematically paired with all the other slopes. Each child saw the 15-degree oblique, for example, compared at different times to the 30-degree, the 45-degree, the 60-degree, and the 75-degree obliques.

There were three main results to this experiment (Table 4.2). First, all the simultaneous comparisons were very easy. Next, the successive comparisons between an oblique and either a horizontal or a vertical

Table 4.2 Mean error scores (out of 20) in second mirror-image experiment (Bryant, 1973)

Con-dition	4 yr		5 yr		6 yr		7 yr	
	Simul-taneous	Succes-sive	Simul-taneous	Succes-sive	Simul-taneous	Succes-sive	Simul-taneous	Succes-sive
OM								
$\bar{X}$	2·00	9·75	0·50	9·50	0·40	6·10	0·35	1·80
SD	3·24	10·26	0·92	9·99	0·80	7·13	0·69	2·43
ONM								
$\bar{X}$	0·85	9·35	0·55	9·65	0·40	5·75	0·55	1·40
SD	2·33	9·87	0·89	10·22	0·92	7·35	0·95	2·00
O/HV								
$\bar{X}$	1·55	2·10	0·45	1·90	0·40	2·10	0·40	0·90
SD	2·98	3·11	1·54	2·70	0·80	3·31	0·63	1·56
HV/O								
$\bar{X}$	0·95	1·85	0·35	1·25	0·35	1·90	0·35	1·00
SD	2·84	3·38	0·69	1·15	0·76	2·94	0·76	1·62

OM = mirror-image obliques; ONM = non mirror-image obliques; O/HV = oblique (St) vs horizontal, or vertical; HV/O = horizontal or vertical (St) vs oblique.

were also very easy for all four age groups. The third result was that all age groups made more errors in the two successive comparisons between obliques than in the other two successive comparisons, and that these errors were as numerous when the two obliques were not mirror-images as when they were.

This makes it virtually certain that the mirror-image analysis is quite wrong, at least as far as young children are concerned. Obliques are difficult because they are obliques. Of course as it stands this is just a negative conclusion, which poses a problem rather than solves it. However, it certainly helps to know exactly what the problem is.

Perceptual frameworks and perceptual inferences

It turns out that a most convenient way to solve the problem is to think in terms of perceptual frameworks. We now have two basic results to deal with: first, young children of four and five years seem to be very well able to make simultaneous orientation matches whatever orientations are involved; secondly difficulties in successive comparisons are quite specific. Children have consistent trouble distinguishing obliques, whatever their slope and as much when they are not mirror-images as when they are. A global theory about children not paying attention to orientation will not cover these two results. If children can manage all simultaneous problems and even some successive problems they are obviously paying attention to orientation. Nor, as we have seen, can a mirror-image analysis explain the specific difficulty with obliques.

A third possibility is that these results could be analysed in terms of some kind of absolute memory store. The hypothesis would be that young children take in the absolute orientations, registering that this line is horizontal and that line a 45-degree oblique pointing in a particular direction, and so on, but that they remember some absolute orientations better than others. They remember horizontals and verticals very well, but forget obliques. This would certainly account for the general discovery that children have more difficulty with successive comparisons between obliques than between horizontals and verticals. However, it would not really explain the very consistent result that in successive comparisons involving choices between an oblique and a horizontal or a vertical choice line, they make very few errors indeed. If children just had poor memories for obliques one would expect them to make more errors in this comparison than in the equivalent comparison between horizontals and verticals: but this is not the case.

Perhaps one could suggest an even more specific absolute theory. However, an alternative approach, which turns out to be much more satisfactory and much more economical, is to argue that children adopt a relative code for orientation, and that this code is suitable for some comparisons but not for others.

The relative hypothesis is a very simple one. Its basic premise is that young children simply register when lines are parallel and when they are not. If the child is shown two lines simultaneously he notices whether their orientations are the same or not. This is the simplest of all possible relative codes, because it has only two 'outputs'. One, which I shall call a 'match' signal, occurs when the child sees parallel lines. The other, a 'mismatch' signal, arises if the lines are not parallel. The code does not register anything about the actual orientations involved. It does not tell the child whether lines are horizontals or obliques, only whether they are oriented in the same way as other lines in the visual field.

This code could explain the discovery that children appear to manage all simultaneous orientation comparisons with ease provided that the display is simple enough. But how would it manage successive comparisons? The answer may lie in the perceptual framework. It can be argued quite plausibly that if children can notice whether two lines are parallel or not, they can also notice whether a line presented on its own parallels features of its background or not. If two lines are parallel to the same background feature, they must be parallel to each other. To use this rule would be one way of solving a successive comparison by making a deductive inference.

Now one of the most obvious things one notices about the usual frame of reference is that the orientations of its main features are not at all random. In this carpentered world, and certainly in the carpentered environment in which experiments on children's perception of orientation have always taken place, there are many vertical and horizontal lines and very few oblique lines. To take one simple example, in most of the experiments, which have been described here, the lines were drawn on square or rectangular cards, whose sides, of course, are vertical or horizontal, and not oblique. So a child using the match–mismatch code and noting when lines paralleled features in their background would register a match when he saw a horizontal or a vertical line and a mismatch whenever he saw an oblique.

We can now consider what implications this would have for the different successive orientation comparisons. First, one would expect that the code would solve a successive comparison between a horizontal and a vertical line because these would match different features of their background. We know now how easy such comparisons are. Secondly, one would expect any successive comparison between an oblique and either a horizontal or a vertical line to be just as easy, because the oblique would produce a mismatch and the horizontal or vertical a match signal. As we have seen, this sort of successive comparison is also an easy one for young children. Thirdly, one would expect that successive comparisons between obliques in whatever orientation would be difficult, for each oblique would produce the same mismatch signal. All that the match–mismatch code will record about an oblique is that it does not parallel anything in the background. If this is all the child remembers about the standard oblique he will not be able to say which of two choice obliques is correct because neither of them parallels anything in the background. Notice that the code would confuse non mirror-image pairs of obliques as much as mirror-image pairs: all that is necessary for a confusion is that none of the obliques presented matches any background feature.

Thus the match–mismatch hypothesis accounts for the fact that successive comparisons between horizontals and verticals or between obliques and horizontals or verticals are easy, while successive comparisons between obliques, asymmetrical as well as symmetrical, are hard for the young child.

It also makes a very simple prediction, which is that young children should be able to solve successive comparisons between obliques if appropriate framework cues are to hand. There is some evidence that this prediction is sound. In one of our earlier experiments (Bryant, 1969, Exp. 3) we found that a diamond surround, whose sides were coloured differently, helped the child to make successive oblique–oblique comparisons while a similar but square surround did not. More recently (Bryant, 1972, Exp. 2) we have found some even more exact signs that children use the match–mismatch code in successive comparisons between obliques.

This experiment was with four-, five-, and six-year-old children, and they were given only successive oblique–oblique problems. These comparisons took three forms. In one the children were given a large white card with an oblique line in the centre of the top half. This was then removed and after an interval of five seconds they were shown another white card at the bottom of which were two obliques side by side and pointing in opposite directions. The children had to choose the line whose orientation was the same as the standard's. This then was a typical successive oblique–oblique comparison and we called it the *no constant cue condition*.

The other two comparisons were also successive and between obliques. However, they both included a framework feature which was present in the card with the standard line and in the card with the choice lines. This framework feature was a thick red line which, as Fig. 4.1 shows, was drawn right across the centre of the card. Its orientation was always the same for each individual child whenever it occurred throughout the session (though its orientation varied between children) and each child was told that the red line always had the same orientation.

In one of the comparisons in which this constant feature occurred it was always parallel to one of the two choice lines. We called this the *appropriate constant cue condition*. In the other comparison, which we called the *inappropriate constant cue condition*, the feature was again present but none of the oblique lines paralleled it. In match–mismatch terms this should mean that in the appropriate condition one choice oblique should produce a match, the other a mismatch signal, and since

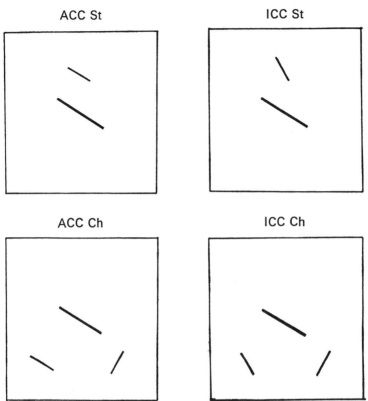

Figure 4.1 Standard and choice cards (Bryant, 1973, Exp. 3)
ACC = appropriate framework
ICC = inappropriate framework
St = standard framework card
Ch = choice card

these two signals are distinguishable the condition should be an easy one. On the other hand, in the inappropriate condition all the obliques should produce the same mismatch signal making the condition as difficult as the usual successive comparison between obliques. Thus the match–mismatch hypothesis predicts that the appropriate condition should be much easier than the other two conditions which should be equally hard.

This was what happened. In all three age groups the children made fewer errors when the constant cue was appropriate than when there was no constant cue. There was no difference between the condition in which the constant cue was 'inappropriate' and the condition in which there was no such cue at all. Table 4.3 shows these results. It seems then that children use framework features when they judge orientation and that they use them in a fairly specific way.

This discovery certainly supports the match–mismatch hypothesis and it is very difficult to see how it can be explained in terms of the other three approaches which were mentioned at the beginning of this section. We have here a very good example of the way children use relative codes to remember something about a specific stimulus. The code does not tell them anything about the absolute properties of the

Table 4.3   Mean error scores (out of 24) in framework experiment (Bryant, 1973), Exp. 3

Age	NCC	ACC	ICC
4 yr			
$\bar{X}$	11·15	5·45	11·05
SD	10·91	6·58	11·71
5 yr			
$\bar{X}$	11·60	5·95	11·95
SD	12·46	6·67	12·46
6 yr			
$\bar{X}$	10·00	2·80	9·45
SD	10·80	3·80	10·50

NCC = no constant cue; ACC = appropriate constant cue;
ICC = inappropriate constant cue.

stimulus but it does tell them about the relationship between the stimulus and its background. When the background cues are appropriate the child can distinguish successively presented stimuli from one another. The very specific errors which occur in the case of orientation are caused by the fact that the child's normal frame of reference is far more suitable for some orientation discriminations than for others.

Even more important is the discovery that the code can work through inferences. When the child compares two things, presented separately, by connecting them through their relationships to some common feature, he is making a perceptual deductive inference. We now have *direct* evidence that young children can make these inferences when they compare orientations.

External and internal categories

The match–mismatch code is an external one. It depends on external relations either between two lines which are compared directly or between a line and some part of its background. The relationship is always between two things which are present together in the immediate environment and if these external relationships are not available the match–mismatch code does not work

This is an important point because it is fairly clear that people who obviously do not depend on the match–mismatch code usually can be shown to be using internal rather than external categories for information about orientation. Perhaps the best evidence for a change from external to internal categories is produced by the Witkin rod and frame experiments described in the first chapter. The younger children tended wrongly to set the luminous line parallel to the tilted luminous framework, when their task was to set this line to true vertical. They were heavily influenced by external framework relations. On the other hand, the older children tended more and more to approximate to true vertical and this developmental change suggests a gradual increase in the effectiveness of internal categories which override the powerful framework cues. Since the room was completely dark apart from the luminous rod and frame, the cues which the older children were using must have been internal ones.

Much the same analysis can be applied to some of the results in our own experiments. When describing these experiments, I dealt almost entirely with the performance of the four- and five-year-olds who typically find successive comparisons between obliques much more difficult than those between a horizontal and a vertical. However, this specific difficulty declines very rapidly with age. In Rudel and Teuber's experiment the eight-year-olds learned the discrimination between obliques very nearly as easily as that between a horizontal and a vertical. Moreover, in one of our experiments (Bryant, 1969, Exp. 1) seven-year-olds made as few errors in a successive comparison between obliques as in one involving horizontals and verticals. Thus by the time they are eight children can remember the orientations of oblique lines even when the background cues are quite inappropriate for a match–mismatch code. It can be suggested quite reasonably that between the ages of four and eight years there is a transition from external to internal categories in orientation perception.

What form do these internal categories take if they are to solve a successive comparison between obliques ? Obviously they must in some way distinguish left from right. The basic difference between two obliques which point in the opposite direction is that the top of one is pointing to the left and of the other to the right. However, the results which have been described so far do not allow us to say anything more specific than this. What form this left–right distinction takes, how it develops, what its causes are, remain at this stage quite obscure. We have to find out more about the way children deal with information about position and particularly how they manage such categories as left and right, up and down, and so on. This will be the purpose of the next chapter.

5

Position

Any object which a child sees has its own position in space, and it is often quite important that he should be able to remember what it is. On the whole it seems that he can remember the positions of individual objects very well.

Some of the evidence is derived from babies. By the age of eight months a baby is able to reach for and find an object which he has seen hidden in a particular position. At this age he tends to get in a muddle if the object is subsequently hidden in another position (Piaget, 1952, 1954; Gratch and Landers, 1971) and so his memory for positions is not entirely effective. However by the age of twelve months these particular errors have disappeared and the baby can search for the object whatever the position in which it was hidden. So when the baby is only one year old he seems to have an efficient way of remembering the positions of individual objects, at least over a short period.

Discrimination learning experiments produce the same sort of conclusion. They show that position is a powerful cue. The easiest discrimination learning task for a young child is a position discrimination (Zeaman and House, 1963). Moreover in discrimination tasks in which position is irrelevant it is quite usual to find the young child responding initially to position before he begins to use the relevant cues. We can be sure then that young children have an effective way of registering and retaining the actual position of an individual object. However, saying this is very like suggesting that children have an effective absolute code for position. If they remember where an individual object is, are they not remembering its absolute position?

This need not be so. It is quite possible to think of a relative code which would record where a thing was, provided it was able to use background relationships. Suppose, for example, that a child leaves a toy on the floor in front of an electric socket in the wall. The toy has an absolute position but it also has a relative position *vis-à-vis* a constant framework feature. Thus the child can register the toy's position either in absolute terms or relatively.

Is there any evidence that children can take in this type of 'in line' position relation? Curiously enough one of the first experiments on the influence of frameworks on children's discrimination of obliques did establish that children were able to notice and remember when one thing is in line with another. This was an experiment by Jeffrey (1958). He worked with children aged around four years and he showed them stick-men whose two arms were stretched out in a continuous oblique line sometimes pointing one way sometimes the other. The children had to discriminate these two obliques successively and naturally found this hard to do. However, when there were two buttons at the top left and right hand corners of the apparatus which were placed in such a way that one oblique was directly in line with and pointing at one button and the other at the other, the discrimination became much easier. The children were trained to press the button with which a particular oblique was in line, and this experience usually led them to discriminate between the successively presented obliques very well.

The basic cue here seems to be an 'in line' one. The obliques were recognized as different because they were in line with different constant features in the background. Perhaps this discovery demonstrates the existence of a basic relative code for position which is rather like the match–mismatch code for orientation described in the last chapter. The position code could also be a binary one with two possible outputs, one that two things are in line, the other that they are out of line. It would also be a match–mismatch code, and could be used inferentially with the help of background cues. The child could remember the position of an individual object simply by recording what feature of the background it lined up with.

The first step in testing such an hypothesis is to examine the way in which children make position comparisons when the in-line out-of-line cue is present, and when it is not.

Simple position comparisons and the in-line /out-of-line cue

One of the simplest ways of testing the young child's ability to take in position relations is to give him a simultaneous two-choice matching task. Let us say that he is shown three squares side by side, and that each square contains a black dot. The only difference between squares is

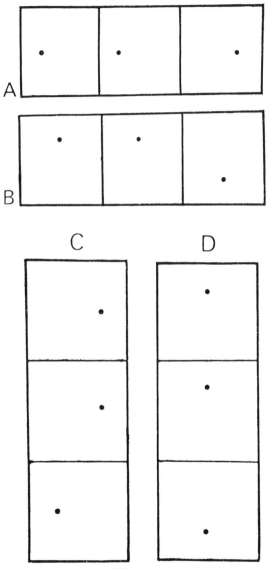

Figure 5.1

in the relative position of each dot in its square, and the child's task is to say which of the two outside squares is identical to the one in the centre. This is therefore a position discrimination.

Figure 5.1 shows four such comparisons. Notice that in two displays (A and C) the relative position of the dots varies from left to right, while in the other two (B and D) the difference is up–down.

We used these four simple comparisons in an experiment on the way five-, six-, and seven-year-old children perceive position (Bryant, 1973, Exp. 3). The children were shown a series of rectangular cards divided by black lines into three equal squares, each of which contained a black dot. Half the time (A and B) the cards were horizontally aligned and the other half vertically, and in every case the child had only to point out which of the two outside squares was the same as the centre one. These were simultaneous matches because the standard and the choice squares were presented together.

The results of this experiment were very clear (Table 5.1). First in the two comparisons in which the squares were aligned horizontally, A

Table 5.1   Mean errors (out of 20) with equal distance position displays (Bryant, 1973)

	5 yr				6 yr				7 yr			
	In line		Out of line		In line		Out of line		In line		Out of line	
	L–R	U–D	L–R	U–D	L–R	U–D	L–R	U–D	L–R	U–D	L–R	U–D
	A	D	C	B	A	D	C	B	A	D	C	B
$\bar{X}$	7·05	6·05	1·65	2·80	5·70	5·35	0·95	1·75	2·80	2·60	0·65	0·95
SD	7·65	6·95	2·48	3·60	6·49	6·54	1·61	2·42	3·28	4·32	1·32	1·76

L–R = left–right; U–D = up–down.

and B, the left–right discrimination, A, was much harder than the up–down one, B, and this at first seems to suggest that left–right relations are harder to take in than up–down ones. However, the pattern of errors made with the two vertically aligned displays, C and D, shows that this is the wrong conclusion. Here the left-right discrimination C was much easier than the up-down one, D. So A and C are consistently easy and B and D are consistently difficult. This difference between A and C on the one hand and B and D on the other, appeared in all three age groups, although the effect was much greater among the five- than the seven-year-olds. Why then are B and C so easy

and A and D so much more difficult for young children of five years or so ?
The most obvious answer is that the two easy displays provide a cue
which the other two displays do not. In the easy comparisons, B and C,
the incorrect dot is plainly out of line with the other two, and the child
can compare the three dots without having to refer to the relative positions (left, right, up and down) of each dot in its own square. All that is
necessary to solve the B and C problems is to note which of the two
outside dots is out of line with the other two.

On the other hand this in-line/out-of-line cue is simply not available
in the other two comparisons, A and D, because the dots are all in line
with each other. The child must take in something about the relative
position of each dot in its own square, and this is apparently quite
difficult. Indeed the performance of the five-year-olds in these two
difficult comparisons was scarcely above chance level, which suggests
that their ability to use relations such as left and right and up and down
is quite severely limited.

So this simple experiment produced two very clear conclusions. The
first is that the in-line/out-of-line relation is an easy one for young
children. The second is that other position relations such as left–right
and up–down are rather difficult. Each of these conclusions raises a
further question of its own. Can the in-line/out-of-line code be used
inferentially through the perceptual framework ? As we have seen it can
plausibly be described as a match–mismatch code. Is it then possible to
make the same kind of inferential comparisons with this code as with the
orientation match–mismatch code ?

A second question which stems from children's difficulties with
left–right and with up–down relations is what exactly this difficulty
involves. The existence of the difficulty, particularly with left–right
relations, is well documented in studies of children's understanding of
spatial relations (Piaget and Inhelder, 1956; Howard and Templeton,
1966) in work on children's difficulties in learning to read (Vernon,
1957; Lieberman, Shankweiler, Orlando and Harris, 1972) and in
traditional intelligence tests. Yet the precise nature of the difficulty
remains obscure. One often suggested possibility is that it has something to do with symmetry and mirror-images.

I shall deal with the second of these questions before coming back to
the first. The reason for taking them in this order is that if the symmetry argument is right, then my description of the in-line/out-of-line
code is probably wrong, because the easy in-line/out-of-line comparisons could more simply be described as non mirror-images.

Symmetry and the in-line comparisons

A glance at the four comparisons which have just been described will show that they fit in very well with the mirror-image analysis. The choice squares in the two difficult comparisons, A and D, are symmetrical around a vertical axis in A and around a horizontal axis in D. On the other hand the choice squares in the two easy comparisons are not symmetrical in this way and are certainly not mirror-images.

In fact, this was precisely the analysis produced to explain the results of some experiments very similar to the one described in the last section. These are the important experiments of Huttenlocher (1967, a, b). It is somewhat churlish of me not to have acknowledged these experiments until now because they provided the basis for my own experiment described in the last section. They have been left to this section because they explicitly raise the question of symmetry.

Huttenlocher's starting point was one of Rudel and Teuber's discrimination tasks (1963). Rudel and Teuber also compared a problem in which children had to learn to respond to one of a pair of figures ⌐ ⌐ which varied from left to right, with another problem in which the difference between the figures was an up–down one, ⊓⊔. Rudel and Teuber found that the left–right discrimination was much more difficult than the up–down one. Huttenlocher observed that there were two possible ways of explaining this. One was that left–right discriminations are easier than up–down ones, and the other that the difficult figures are symmetrical around the vertical axis, while the easy ones are not. In her tasks, which involved in one case (1967, a) discrimination learning and in another (1967, b) a form of simultaneous matching, Huttenlocher used four pairs of figures, (a) ⌐ ⌐, (b) ⊓⊔, (c) ⌐, and (d) ⊓. These, of course, are respectively very similar to my A, B, C, and D displays, and indeed mine were derived directly from Huttenlocher's. Huttenlocher's results also were very similar to mine. The left–right discrimination was much more difficult when the figures were placed symmetrically around the vertical axis, (a), than when they were not (c). Similarly many more errors were made with the up–down discrimination in which the figures involved were symmetrical around the horizontal axis, (d), than in the one in which they were placed asymmetrically, (b).

Huttenlocher analysed these results in terms of mirror-images. However, there is an alternative analysis, which is essentially the same as the one which I have given for the experiment in which children matched the positions of dots. The alternative is that the easy discriminations are easy because they are characterized by the easy in-line/out-of-line cue. To tell that ⊓⊓ are the same and ⊓⊔ different, and also that ⌐ are the same and ¬ different can simply be done by noting whether in the first two pairs the distinctive horizontal lines and in the second the distinctive vertical lines are in- or out-of-line with each other. However, the difficult discriminations are difficult because this easy cue is not present. The distinctive vertical line is in-line both when the figures ⌐⌐ are the same and when they are different ⌐ ¬. The same goes for the distinctive horizontal line in the other difficult comparison, since this is as much in line when the two figures are different, ⊓⊔, as when they are not, ⊓⊓. So according to this alternative analysis the easy discriminations are really in-line/out-of-line discriminations, and the difficult ones are difficult because they do not provide this easy cue, and have to be solved by noting whether particular lines are to the left or right, or up or down.

The major difference between Huttenlocher's analysis and this one, apart from the new idea of the in-line/out-of-line code, is over the question of the importance of symmetry. According to my analysis symmetry has nothing to do with the number of errors made in the difficult comparisons. These comparisons are simple in-line comparisons which have to be solved on the basis of left–right differences or up–down differences. Young children have difficulty coding these kinds of differences, and they have as much difficulty when the displays are asymmetrical as when they are symmetrical, provided the displays do not offer the in-line/out-of-line cue.

One way of sorting out whether symmetry is as important as Huttenlocher suggests is to introduce displays which are in-line, but asymmetrical. Her approach would have to predict that these would be easier than the symmetrical displays, while mine would predict that they would be as difficult. However, the trouble with Huttenlocher's figures is that they do not allow this kind of control: if you make her figures asymmetrical you also change their shape, which of course introduces another cue.

This actually is the major advantage of our dot comparisons, because it is quite easy to change the in-line comparisons, so that sometimes they are asymmetrical, without having to change the shape of the figures involved. The dot is still only a dot. Suppose, for example, that in the left–right discrimination, A, the choice dot whose position is to the left of its square is 2 inches to the left of the midpoint of its square, and that the choice dot which is on the right of its square is 2 inches to the right: this is a symmetrical comparison, and a mirror-image one. However, if, for example, the left choice dot is only $\frac{1}{2}$ inch to the left of its square's midpoint while the right one is 2 inches off the midpoint, then this comparison is definitely not a mirror-image one because the choice squares are not symmetrical.

This control was included in the experiment with dot patterns which has already been described (Bryant, 1972, Exp. 3). Each of the three squares was 6 inches in width, so that the distance between midpoint and the sides of the square was 3 inches. The distance of the dot from its midpoint, that is to say the extent to which it was to the left or to the right or above or below the centre of the square, was varied. There were five possible distances of the dot from its midpoint, $2\frac{1}{2}$ inches, 2 inches, $1\frac{1}{2}$ inches, 1 inch, and $\frac{1}{2}$ inch. These distances were varied in such a way that each child was given all four comparisons under two conditions. In one of these, all three dots were an equal distance from the midpoint of the square, so that, for example, if one choice dot was $2\frac{1}{2}$ inches above midpoint the other was $2\frac{1}{2}$ inches below. The results for this condition were given in the last section (Table 5.1). In the other condition the distance of the two choice dots from the midpoints of their squares was different so that one choice might be $2\frac{1}{2}$ inches above and the other only $\frac{1}{2}$ inch below its midpoint.

The crucial question here concerns what happens in the two in-line comparisons A and D. An analysis such as Huttenlocher's, which is based on the symmetry of the confused figures, would have to predict that the equal distance condition would cause more errors in the in-line comparisons, A and D, than the unequal distance condition. On the other hand the hypothesis which I have been arguing for would predict that A and D would be equally difficult in both conditions because they do not offer the in-line/out-of-line cue.

The result was that symmetry had no effect whatsoever (Table 5.2). It seems then that once again the mirror-image question has turned out to be a blind alley.

We also have evidence from one other experiment with five-year-old children (Bryant, 1970) that the mirror-image analysis is unsatisfactory, and this experiment provides as well an interesting example of how the young child's orientation and position codes are interrelated.

Table 5.2 Mean errors (out of 20) with unequal distance position displays (Bryant, 1973)

	5 yr				6 yr				7 yr			
	In line		Out of line		In line		Out of line		In line		Out of line	
	L–R	U–D	L–R	U–D	L–R	U–D	L–R	U–D	L–R	U–D	L–R	U–D
	A	D	C	B	A	D	C	B	A	D	C	B
$\bar{X}$	6·75	6·65	2·05	1·50	5·70	5·60	0·85	0·55	3·15	2·60	0·65	1·15
SD	7·49	7·61	2·91	2·41	6·45	6·84	1·52	0·95	3·64	4·17	1·32	1·99

The experiment involved the three displays in Fig. 5.2. If we consider the three displays from the point of view of the mirror-image question we can see that the choices in E and in F are mirror-images. Again it is the child's task to select the outside figure which is the same as the centre one, and in E and F the two choice figures are mirror-images in that they are symmetrical around the vertical axis. On the other hand, in

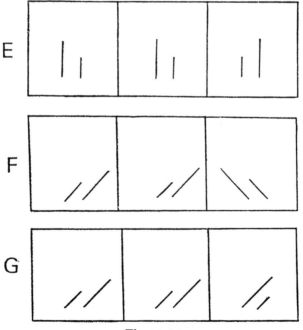

Figure 5.2

these terms the choices in G are not. So from the mirror-image point of view E and F should be equally difficult, and G should be much easier.

However, one reaches quite a different set of predictions with the match–mismatch hypothesis. This predicts that F should be much easier than E. E does not offer the in-line/out-of-line cue. The distinctive features are in line with one another, and the lines are parallel. To solve this problem the child must use something like a left–right code, and thus the comparison should be as difficult as the A and D comparison described earlier. On the other hand, the figures which have to be discriminated in F are not parallel, and the child has the basis for an orientation match–mismatch comparison. Finally figures in G should be rather too difficult to discriminate on a match–mismatch basis. The distinctive lines are in line and they are again parallel in G. There is therefore, as in D, no basis for a match–mismatch comparison.

When these displays were given to five-year-old children – and to severely subnormal adults – (Bryant, 1970), the results were very much as predicted by the match–mismatch hypothesis. The difficult displays were E and G, and they were as difficult as each other. On the other hand the F display was very much easier and young children and severely subnormal adults made relatively few errors despite the fact that it was a mirror-image comparison. So it seems that what determines the difficulty of these discriminations has nothing very much to do with the question of symmetry. It is much more a matter of whether or not they are appropriate for a match–mismatch code. They are not appropriate for this sort of code when the lines are parallel and when the distinctive features are in line.

Two points can be made about these experiments. The first is that once again symmetry in the display has been shown not to be a major cause of perceptual confusions in young children. The basic fact which has emerged is that the young child has difficulty registering whether something is to the left or the right, but that this does not mean that he will be confused only about figures which are left–right mirror-images. The child who has difficulty registering left and right will tend to confuse any pair of obliques (in successive presentation) and also any left–right or up–down patterns which do not offer the direct in-line/out-of-line cue, whether or not these line and dot displays are mirror-images.

If one reflects a while one can also see that some of the reasons for suggesting that the symmetry in the display might be important are rather odd. Take, for example, Orton's analysis which was in terms of the symmetry of the two cerebral hemispheres. His major argument, it will be recalled, was that the confusions arose between mirror-images because every single shape which a person sees produces mirror-image patterns of excitation in the two hemispheres. But surely this can only be a problem if there is a little man in the head sitting astride the corpus callosum, looking from one hemisphere to the other. It may indeed be that when I see one object it produces mirror-image patterns in my left and right hemispheres, but this does not mean that I see the object and its mirror-image at the same time, any more than I see the world upside-down because that is the way it is represented on my retina. Provided that the object produces one pattern and its mirror-image another distinctive pattern in each hemisphere, as even Orton's theory admits it does, it matters not one jot whether the patterns of firing in the two hemispheres are mirror-images.

This is very clearly a conceptual confusion between the person's physical symmetry and the symmetry of the perceptual display. It is probably quite true, as Mach originally suggested, that young children do have difficulty in registering left–right differences because the symmetry of their own body does not give them a sound basis for an internal left–right category. It is probably also true that, when for one reason or another, internal asymmetries develop, children are in a much better position to tell left from right. However, we now know that the difficulty which young children have in using a left–right relational code leads them to confusions between asymmetrical figures as much as between symmetrical figures. The cerebral hemispheres may be mirror-images, but that does not mean that the child as a result confuses only mirror-image figures.

The second point is that these results seem to confirm the suggestion that a major difference between easy and difficult position comparisons is whether or not they provide the in-line/out-of-line cue. This cue is a powerful one, and can be used very effectively by young children. It is obviously a relative cue for position, since it tells the child not exactly where an object is, but how its position relates to something else's position. Since my argument has been that children use relative codes inferentially with the help of background framework features, the next question must be whether this particular position code is also applied to constant background cues.

Perceptual frameworks and inferences about position

If the binary match–mismatch codes for orientation and for position work in the same way, one would expect that the child would use the information that an object is in line with some framework feature in much the same way as he uses the information that a line parallels a particular part of the framework. He should be able to manage discriminations which normally cause him difficulty if he is given the appropriate framework cues.

Moreover, if he does use framework cues to solve position discriminations he will again be making a perceptual inference. He will be working out, for example, that because both the standard dot and one of the choice dots line up with a constant feature, they must occupy the same position in their respective squares. Doing this he is combining two relations to produce a new relative judgement and this is a deductive inference.

The obvious test is to go back to the difficult comparisons which do not offer the in-line/out-of-line cue and to introduce a constant framework feature. Figure 5.3 shows how this can be done. Here are two new versions of each of the two difficult displays used in the earlier experiments. In each of the three squares in every display there is a red dot (symbolized by r). This red dot is always in the same position with respect of its own square in each of the three squares. In A1, in which the dots which have to be compared vary from left to right, one choice dot lines up with the red reference dot along this left–right axis and the other does not. When the correct choice lines up with the red dot so also does the standard; and when the incorrect choice lines up with it the standard does not. The same applies to D1 except that the axis is vertical. If a child who cannot normally solve the A or the D comparisons (Fig. 5.1) nevertheless manages these new comparisons to which a common reference point has been added, he is probably making an indirect inferential comparison.

We gave these displays to groups of five-year-old children and of severely subnormal adults (Bryant, 1970). In this experiment there were three types of simultaneous comparison. In the first no framework was present and the displays were simply those used in the first experiment described in this chapter (Fig. 5.1). In the second we showed the children displays with the red reference point, arranged in such a way that one choice dot lined up with the reference point and the other did not (Fig. 5.2). In the third the reference point was again there, but none of

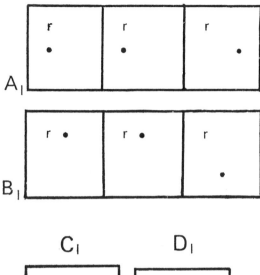

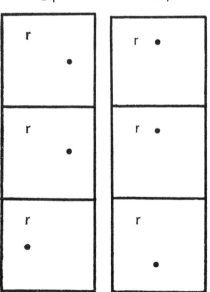

Figure 5.3

the dots which had to be compared lined up with it. This condition served as a control to ensure that the reference point did not improve the position comparisons through some non-specific crowding effect.

The severely subnormal adults produced very much the same pattern of scores as the young children. Both groups did better when one choice dot lined up with the reference point and the other did not, than in the other two conditions. This result suggests that both groups were using a framework feature to help them make position comparisons which otherwise would be quite difficult for them. Moreover, their use of this

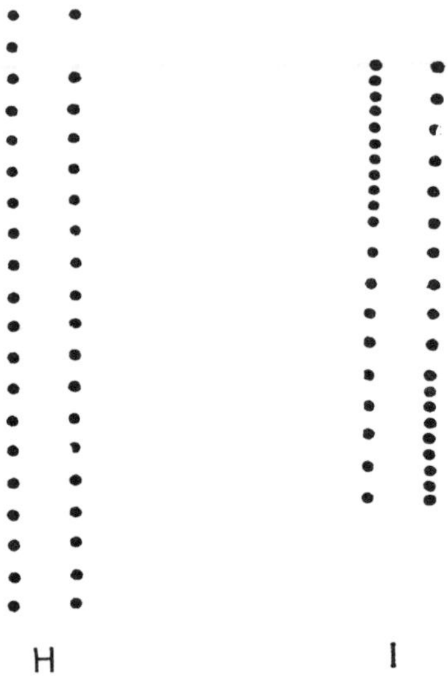

H   I

Figure 5.4

feature is inferential, in that it involves working out that two things are the same because they have the same relation to the same common feature.

We can conclude that the young child may deal with information about orientation and about position in a remarkably similar manner. The codes which he adopts for orientation are both probably relative, they both probably operate primarily in a binary match–mismatch manner, and they both take advantage of framework features with the help of perceptual inferences.

The discovery of the in-line/out-of-line code has two further interesting implications. The first is that the code can be directly linked to the way children compare numbers before they learn how to count. Suppose that the four-year-old is given a task in which he has to judge which of two parallel rows of counters has more in it. Figure 5.4 shows two possible displays, H and I. It has been known for some time that young children are much more likely to be correct with the display like H than with the other display. The reason is that there is a spatial one-to-one correspondence in H between the two rows, which are arranged like two ranks of soldiers, and that this cue is not present in I. Now this spatial one-to-one correspondence can be described in in-line terms. The correspondence exists because each counter in the two rows is in line with a particular counter in the other row, except for one counter in the more numerous row, which has no counterpart. Thus it may be that the child's position codes are directly linked to the way he judges number. This, and other early number codes, will be discussed in Chapter 7.

The second implication of the in-line/out-of-line code is a practical one. It has already been noted that children who are beginning to learn to read may have difficulty in knowing from which direction to start reading words and lines. The problem simply is whether to go from left to right or from right to left. There seems to be some uncertainty still about how important a problem this is for those children who are having difficulty with reading (Vernon, 1971). However, there is no reason why the problem should not be overcome at least at first by using a simple marker. The child who does not know from which direction to start reading but can use framework cues will surely be helped by having a prominent marker, such as a red line drawn down the left hand side of each page, to tell him that this is the side which should be his starting point. This is an idea which could be very easily tested, and a simple experiment like this might very well have some practical significance.

So work on position discriminations may be relevant to the study of how a child learns to read, and this may be another link between the orientation and the position experiments. There is, however, one striking difference between the two sets of experiment, which is important for any general discussion of relative codes. It concerns the distinction between simultaneous and successive comparisons.

Perception, memory and the match–mismatch codes

One problem about the experiments on children's perception of orientation is that all the young children's difficulties were in simultaneous comparisons which involved memory. Yet the match–mismatch hypothesis put forward to explain these errors was basically about the way the child handles the perceptual input at the time when it arrives. The problem is that it is a little awkward to base a theory about the handling of perceptual input on patterns of errors made in tasks which also involve memory.

There was, of course, a perfectly good reason for this use of evidence. A match–mismatch orientation code should solve all simultaneous comparisons because when lines are presented together the code will detect which are parallel and which not. Therefore the code can only lead to errors in successive situations, and according to the hypothesis these errors should crop up when the perceptual framework for one reason or another is not suitable. The hypothesis can only be tested by patterns of errors in successive tasks.

Thus with the perception of orientation there is no way round the difficulty of looking at perception through tasks which involve memory. Fortunately this dilemma does not also apply to the closely similar match–mismatch hypothesis about young children's perception of position. This hypothesis predicts errors in some simultaneous comparisons, since it is possible to devise simultaneous position comparisons which do not provide the match–mismatch, in-line/out-of-line cue. In fact these predicted errors do by and large occur. All the evidence in this chapter was produced by experiments in which standard and choice figures or squares were presented together. We now have direct evidence which supports a match–mismatch code from perceptual experiments where the memory element has almost certainly been eliminated.

Relative theories are inevitably theories about perception as well as about memory. They can always be tested in tasks which involve memory. Sometimes, as in these experiments on the perception of position, they can also be tested in experiments which genuinely do not.

6

Size

In this chapter we return to the continuum of size. It has already been shown that young children respond to and remember relative sizes much more easily than absolute ones (Chap. 2) and that they can co-ordinate separate size relations inferentially (Chap. 3). However, there are two issues which still need discussion. The first concerns the type of relations which children code and the second their understanding of the invariance of size.

The type of relation which was discussed in the chapters on orientation and position perception was very simply a same–different (match–mismatch) relation. This kind of binary relation is arguably the simplest available. At any rate it is by no means the only kind, a fact which is amply illustrated by some of the work which has already been mentioned on the way children deal with size relations.

We have seen that children do quite well in a task in which they must remember always to respond to the larger or to the smaller of two objects even though the absolute sizes of these objects change from trial to trial. They remember a relation and this involves more than just noticing that the two sizes are different. Children notice a direction also. They register and remember which object is the larger. The distinction here, for example, is between on the one hand taking in only that two lines are not parallel, and on the other hand noticing that two squares have different sizes and in addition which one is the larger. Both codes are relative, but the size code gives the direction of the relation, while the orientation code does not.

Some of this is speculation and some of it is not. We do not know for certain that the child's relative orientation codes only operate on a same–different basis, without telling him about the direction of the difference. That is only my hypothesis, although it is very difficult to conceive of a truly relative code for orientation which could produce information about the direction of a difference. However, we definitely do know from the experiments reviewed in Chapter 2 that children can take in and remember the directions of size differences. Yet this certain data itself raises new questions. What does it mean exactly to say that the young child remembers that the red square was larger than the blue one? Is this all he notices or does he also note that the red one is precisely twice as large as the blue? This further distinction is between remembering an all or nothing relation ('larger than') and remembering a ratio ('twice as large as').

The second issue, which is about invariance, is closely related to the first. As we move around our environment the size of the image of a particular object which we see will vary. As we approach its retinal size will grow, and as we retreat it will shrink. Yet we understand that the object's actual size has stayed the same, and the problem is how we do this. One possible approach to this problem, often called the problem of constancy, fits in well with the sort of theory being advanced in this book. We may solve the problem of constancy by ignoring absolute changes in the size of the retinal image and concentrating instead on the relationships between the object in question and its surrounding framework.

For example, the book which I have spotted and want to read and which is on the bookshelves at the other side of my room takes up a certain proportion of the distance between the shelf it stands on and the shelf above. The book produces a tiny retinal image in my eye when I see it from across the room. If I get up and walk over to the shelves to collect the book its retinal image will grow very radically. However, the relation of the size of the book to the size of its surrounds will stay constant. The ratio between the height of the book and the distance between the shelves will always be constant. If I rely on the relation between an object and its background I have a good basis for realizing that the object's size is invariant despite changes in its retinal size.

There is some evidence that people do use framework cues as a basis for understanding the stability of the sizes of objects around them. This will be discussed in some detail later on in this chapter. At the moment it is worth pointing out that if people do use these framework cues they must be responding not just in general to size relations but more specifically to size ratios. If I notice that the size of something on my bookshelves is constant on the basis of the fact that its relation to the distance between shelves below and above it has remained the same, I must be acting on the basis of a size ratio. I could not simply use an all or nothing relation which would tell me that the distance between the two shelves is greater than the height of the object. That information would be too imprecise because if the object's size actually did change somehow and got smaller, its height would still be smaller than the distance between shelves. On the other hand, noting the ratio of the object's size to the size of its surrounds will help distinguish whether the object's actual size has stayed constant or not.

Thus the two issues which have been raised now in a rather preliminary way are connected. If a child or an adult can register and remember a ratio he should be able to use the perceptual framework to help him work out when sizes are constant and when they are not. The first question to settle therefore is whether children, whom we already know can take in relations like 'larger' and 'smaller', can manage size ratios as well.

Children's perception of size ratios

Usually great care is taken in the typical transposition experiment (of the sort described at length in Chap. 2) to keep the ratio between sizes precisely the same in all the pairs of sizes used in the experiment. If one of the sizes in the training pair is twice that of the other, then one size will be twice as large as the other in all the transposition tests as well. Usually the ratios are rather more pernickety than this. Thus in Spence's (1937) original experiment the ratio between the two sizes in every pair, large and small, training and test, near and far, was 1.6:1. The constant and invariable ratio was 1.8 : 1 in the Kuenne experiment (1946), and 2.6 : 1 in the Johnson and Zara (1960) experiment. In the Lawrenson and Bryant (1972) study, Kuenne's sizes and ratios were adopted.

This insistence on ratios is not intrinsically necessary if one only wants to find out whether children can take in and remember overall relations like larger and smaller. To take just one other possibility, one could arrange things so that the difference between the two sizes in every pair is, for example, 1 square inch. This would mean that the ratio between the two sizes would vary from pair to pair.

The reasons for this insistence on ratio steps rather than any other kind of step are rather obscure. It would not matter much if the absolute hypothesis had been proved, because the question is simply one of how one orders the relations. However, when one finds that there is good evidence for relative responding, then it is clear that the exclusive use of ratio differences leaves some important questions unanswered.

There are at least two outstanding questions here. One is whether the children who do definitely respond relatively are responding to an overall relation like 'larger' which would be transferred to any pair of different sizes whatever their ratio, or whether they are responding to a specific ratio like 1 : 1.5 which could only apply to other pairs with the same ratio difference. Once this question is posed the answer to it seems obvious. It is most unlikely that a young child would bother to go to the lengths of doing anything as complicated as recording a ratio like 1 : 1.5, when they can solve the task simply by remembering something as simple as that the larger object is correct. However, one still cannot exclude the possibility that, for example, in the Lawrenson and Bryant (1972) experiment the children who learned the relational task successfully did so by learning a ratio.

The second unanswered question is whether children can respond to ratios at all. Let us assume for the moment that the common-sense answer to the first question is right and that children who solve a size discrimination on a relative basis normally do so by remembering an overall direction rather than a ratio. We still would not know whether these children could take in information about ratios if they had to. The question is an important one because, as the previous section showed, a child (or an adult) who uses background cues to judge the invariance of an object's size is to some extent recording a ratio.

The first of these questions is very easily answered by giving children relative tasks like those used in the Lawrenson and Bryant experiment except that size ratio is made to vary. The child would be given a discrimination learning task with two pairs with variable size differences, each pair being presented on half the trials and in a random order. In a recent experiment (Lawrenson and Bryant, unpublished) some four-year-old children were given a 'variable ratio' and others a 'constant ratio' relative task. Half of each of these did a 'near' task, the other half a 'far' task. (See Chap. 2 for a discussion of near and far tasks.) No difference was found between any of the tasks. Certainly there was no sign at all that a constant ratio helps children learn a relative task. This result suggests very strongly that when they can be, children are content with remembering simply the direction of a relation.

The answer to the second question is absorbing: it seems very likely that young children can take in and remember size ratios, but in a rather limited way.

This was demonstrated in another recent experiment (Lawrenson and

Bryant, unpublished) with four-year-old children, who were all given a successive matching task which could only be solved by their remembering a ratio. This experiment involved shapes like the one in Fig. 6.1 which were clearly divided into a red and a green part. Each part was as

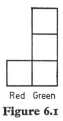

Red Green

Figure 6.1

clearly divided into a certain number of segments which looked rather like bricks piled up one on top of the other, and the actual number of these segments varied from one to four. The number of segments in each of the two differently coloured parts differed, and therefore the

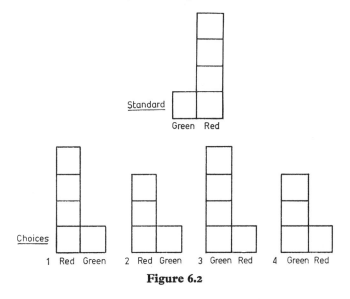

Figure 6.2

heights of the parts were always unequal. This meant that each stimulus could be described either in simple relative terms or as a ratio. Does the child simply remember that the red bit is larger than the green bit? Or does he in some way register that it is four times as large?

This can be tested in a successive matching task. All one has to do is to show the child a figure like this and then later give him some other figures which also are divided into red and green parts, asking him which of these is most like the one which he saw earlier. Figure 6.2 shows how this can be done.

Here the standard which the child sees on its own has a red part which is four times as large as its green part. So the standard has a simple relation (red larger) and a ratio (red four times as large). Two of the four choice stimuli (1 and 2) are characterized by the simple relation, but only one of these, 1, has the correct ratio as well. The other two stimuli are plainly incorrect since in both the green part is taller than the red.

So if the child remembers only a simple relation, he should choose either 1 or 2 very much more often than 3 and 4, and should choose 1 and 2 equally often. If, on the other hand, he remembers something about the ratio as well, he should choose 1 most often. Our experiment involved several trials for each child. Different standards were used so that sometimes the red half was larger, other times the green. The correct ratio also varied from trial to trial. We even varied the absolute size of standard and choice figures, so that in some cases all the choice figures were completely different in absolute size from the standard.

The experiment showed quite clearly that four-year-old children can take in information about ratios as well as about relations, even when the absolute sizes of the choice figures and the standard figure are quite different. In the example given in Fig. 6.2, the children tended to choose 1 much more than 2, although they also chose 2 more than either 3 or 4. So they do recognize ratios although they do not recognize them perfectly. It is also interesting that when they fail to remember the ratio they are more likely to choose a figure with the same simple relation.

Of course, it could be argued against this conclusion that when the children made the correct choice they did so not in response to a ratio but in response to a shape. The shapes of the standard and correct choice are the same. Now this is a very interesting objection, and there are two things one can say about it.

The first is that the only reason why the shapes of the correct and incorrect figures are different is that the ratio between red and green parts differ. So to dismiss this use of ratios as mere shape perception would be quite wrong. However, the second point is that the question of shape does have some significance because it is possible also to produce two figures whose ratios are the same, but whose shapes are quite different. Figure 6.3 shows how this can be done with the sorts of figures which I have been describing. Is it possible for young children to recognize a ratio even when the shape is different?

We gave the same four-year-old children successive comparisons like these, in which the shape of all the choice figures was different from that of the standard. Otherwise the procedure was the same as when the shapes of the correct figure and the standard were the same.

Rather surprisingly even in this condition the children made more ratio choices than one would expect by chance and chose the figure with

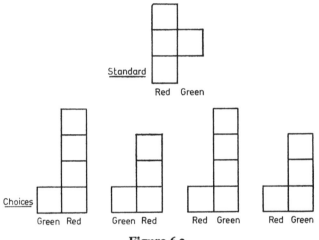

Figure 6.3

the correct ratio more often than the one with the same red–green relation but a different ratio. However the proportion of ratio responses was not nearly so high in this type of comparison as when the shapes of the standard and the correct choice were the same.

We can conclude again that young children can take in ratios to some extent. We can also conclude that there may be two different levels at which ratios are coded. One code depends on the shape being the same, while the other is more sophisticated and can be applied to an infinite number of configurations. The distinction is an intriguing one. One point to note is that if a child is using background cues to help him understand that an object's size is invariant, the more primitive of these two ratios will do. If the book on my shelf stays the same size as I approach it or retreat from it, its ratio to its background will remain constant but so also will the shape of the configuration made by the book in combination with its background. I do not have to register a book-to-shelf ratio which can then be applied to an infinite number of differently shaped configurations.

Another point that should be made about the distinction between the two kinds of ratio is that the more sophisticated type might very well depend on the existence of some kind of absolute code for number. It may be that the child can only manage the kind of ratio which is entirely independent of perceptual configurations by counting the segments. If they do count and realize that there are, for example, four segments to the red and one to the green part, they will have a perfectly good basis for transferring this four to one ratio to whatever shape they come across. Thus here we have an interesting suggestion of an interaction between relative and absolute codes. At first the child can respond to ratios which are restricted to specific perceptual configurations. Later he develops an absolute number code. This code makes it possible for him to respond to the more abstract type of ratio. The question of the development of absolute codes for number and its effects will be discussed in detail in the next chapter.

Now that we know that the child takes in the more primitive type of ratio and thus has a basis for recognizing that the actual sizes of objects around him are invariant even though the sizes of their retinal images change, we can ask whether there is any evidence that people do normally register the ratios of objects to their background.

Framework effects in comparisons of size

The suggestion that people might notice these ratios has been made in this book in two completely different contexts. One involved the invariance of size and the question of size constancy.

The other concerned the explanation of the 'distance effect'. In Chapter 2 it was suggested that young children take in two kinds of relation in a size discrimination task, the relation between the two sizes and the ratio of these sizes to their background. The hypothesis was that young children fail to transpose to a 'far' transposition test because this 'far' test involves a large change in the relations with the background, which upsets them. Again, this relation with the background which they are supposed to remember will be a ratio. It must be a ratio and not an overall relation because all the sizes involved were smaller than their background, and thus had the same overall relation to it. The hypothesis can only work by suggesting that the distance effect is caused by an abrupt change in the ratio between the objects and their backgrounds. However, both these suggestions are still just suggestions, and we obviously need some direct evidence.

There is surprisingly little information about the influence of perceptual frames of reference on the way people make judgements about size. Certainly there is very much more information about framework effects on children's perception of orientation and position than on their perception of size. However, there is one very interesting and important series of experiments, albeit with adults, which demonstrates a very powerful framework effect in comparisons of size, and also provides a very good link between the question of the perceptual frame of reference and the problem of size constancy. These are the experiments of Rock and Ebenholtz (1959), who were interested in the way people compare the absolute lengths of two vertical lines, when these are enclosed in rectangular frameworks whose sizes are quite different. They experimented with a display of two rectangular frameworks, one three times as large as the other, and asked their subjects to set one vertical line so that its absolute size was the same as the other's, notwithstanding the difference in the size of the two frameworks.

Rock and Ebenholtz carried out their experiments in a dark room, with luminous figures. Thus, the only visible framework cue for each vertical line was its rectangular surround. One of the vertical lines was constant and the observer was asked to adjust the other until both were exactly the same length. He was not told to pay attention to the framework and indeed in one experiment the explicit instructions were to ignore the framework and to concentrate on the lines themselves.

These experiments showed very clearly that the frame of reference influences judgements about size. The typical response took the form of a compromise between a correct ratio judgement and a correct absolute judgement. This is certainly a remarkable result for at least two reasons. One is that even when the people were actually instructed not to make ratio judgements, they were still influenced by the lines' relations to their backgrounds. The other is that this error was made even when they knew perfectly well that the two displays were equidistant from them.

There seems to be no other way of explaining this evidence than by accepting the conclusion that our tendency to notice the ratio of the size of the object to its background is so powerful and so ingrained that we cannot entirely overcome it, even when we are asked to and even when we realize that it might distort our judgements. Since children depend so heavily on background cues when they judge orientation and position it is very likely that they might also produce much the same behaviour as Rock and Ebenholtz discovered in adults. Certainly these experiments should be done with young children. In the meantime we can conclude at least that adults may depend very heavily on framework cues when they consider the sizes of individual objects.

The next question is whether these background ratios are used as a basis for understanding the constancy of objects whose retinal sizes fluctuate. Are framework effects the solution to the problem of constancy? The answer to this question is a somewhat complex one, because the traditional experiments on constancy are themselves very complex.

The problem of size constancy

Size constancy experiments are also about the way people judge size, specifically the size of the same object from different distances. Size constancy experiments invariably study this question by investigating the way in which an observer compares the sizes of two objects placed at different distances from him.

The question of the distance of the object from the observer is important because obviously the absolute size of the retinal image alone is no basis on which to judge the actual size of an object; one has to consider what other factors the observer takes into account. The central problem in size constancy experiments has always been how people manage to avoid depending entirely on the size of the retinal image.

There are two basic ways in which one can tackle the problem and both have been tried in constancy experiments. One way, the more obvious, is to show somebody two identical objects at different distances and to ask him to compare their objective sizes. If he can judge correctly, he is obviously using more than just the sizes of the objects' retinal images. Thus one can examine in a fairly simple experiment how well a person does make these objective comparisons, and by what means. This can be called the *objective size constancy experiment*.

The other way is less obvious but in many ways more interesting. It involves asking the person to compare two objects solely on the basis of their retinal sizes. Typically the subject is shown two objects at different distances, but this time he is asked to ignore their objective sizes and their relative distance, and simply to judge how much space they take up in his eye. If a person is looking at two squares, one twice as far away as the other, and if both squares produce the same retinal size, then the further away one will of course be much the larger of the two in objective terms. Thus this type of constancy experiment, which we can call *the retinal size constancy experiment*, tests how well people can confine themselves wholly to retinal sizes when they try to.

One of the reasons why this distinction between the two types of experiment – a distinction very rarely made in the literature – is important is that the term 'constancy' is used in quite different ways in the objective and the retinal experiments. In the objective experiments constancy refers to the observer's success in avoiding being trapped by the object's retinal size. If he manages to judge the objective sizes of objects at different distances from him correctly, he is said to be showing constancy. If he actually overestimates the further object he is said to be showing overconstancy. In 'retinal' constancy experiments, on the other hand, constancy is measured by failure, by unwitting attention to objective sizes despite instructions to ignore them.

The connexion between these two types of experiment is that both measure the strategy for avoiding complete dependence on size of the retinal image, and of basing judgements on the real sizes of objects. Not surprisingly the different types of instructions produce quite different patterns of performance, a difference which is most clearly shown in experiments such as those of Gilinsky (1955) who asked people at different times to make objective and retinal comparisons. Sometimes it is suggested that results like Gilinsky's show that 'attitude' affects 'constancy' (Forgus, 1966). This, however, is probably far too abstract. If you ask people to do different things they almost certainly will behave differently.

Constancy experiments and the absolute–relative question

Having made the distinction between the two kinds of experiments, we can ask which of the two is most relevant to the central theme of the book, the role of relative codes and perceptual inferences. The answer is that the most direct link between the evidence on relational codes for size and the constancy question is through the 'retinal' experiments. This is because the best evidence we have for these codes is the discovery by Rock and Ebenholtz (1959) that adults asked to compare the sizes of two lines took into account the relationship of each line to its surrounds, even when instructed not to.

The link is simple. Let us suppose for the moment that people depend very heavily on an object's surrounds when they judge its objective size, and that they realize that this size is constant even when its retinal image varies because its relations to these surrounds remain constant. This would mean that a person asked to compare objects on the basis of their retinal sizes is really being told to ignore the relationship between object and surrounds. Now Rock and Ebenholtz's experiments seem to have shown that people cannot completely ignore framework relationships even when they try. So one would predict on the basis of a framework hypothesis that people would also fail to make retinal size comparisons perfectly in the retinal constancy experiment. Moreover, one would predict that if they failed to ignore these framework cues they would tend to overestimate the retinal size of the further object.

Suppose that someone is asked to compare the retinal sizes of two squares which are placed at different distances along a table. Suppose too that they are arranged in such a way that from the observer's point of view the two squares produce equal retinal sizes, meaning, of course, that the further square is objectively the larger and also meaning that the relation between the two squares and their common surrounds is quite different. The framework for both is the table, each square occupying a certain ratio of the width of this table. The further square takes up a much greater proportion of the table than the nearer even though their retinal sizes are the same. The observer is asked to ignore this cue and concentrate instead on the squares themselves. If he fails, then he will also tend to overestimate the retinal size of the further object. However, Rock and Ebenholtz's results were 'compromise' results. People who were shown two lines, one of which was in a framework three times as large as the other's, tended to judge the lines as equal when the one in the larger framework was twice as long as the one in the smaller framework. From this compromise one would predict that the retinal judgements in a constancy experiment would also be a compromise, between objective and retinal size. Rock and Ebenholtz showed that adults neither completely depend on nor completely ignore framework cues when they are instructed to. If framework cues are to be used as an explanation of retinal constancy experiments then one would expect that to some extent adults would be able to judge retinal size as instructed, but that to some extent also they would be affected by the relationship between the object and its surrounds and therefore by its objective size.

We can now turn to the experiments themselves, and we find that these universally produce the compromise result one would expect from this framework hypothesis. On the whole, people find it extremely difficult to make correct retinal comparisons of size in retinal constancy experiments, and on the whole they tend to overestimate the size of the further object. Retinal size constancy experiments have a long history, but their results have been remarkably consistent. We can take as an example the earliest, conducted by Thouless (1931).

He asked each person to compare the retinal sizes of two circular discs which were placed at different distances along a table. Naturally the further disc was objectively larger than the nearer one: but the instructions were to compare not their objective sizes but their retinal sizes. The position of the further disc was fixed, while the nearer could be pushed to and fro until the observer decided on the exact position at which the retinal size of the two discs was the same.

In this sort of set-up it is quite possible for the experimenter to calculate geometrically at what point the nearer object produces the same retinal image as the further one, and so he can work out whether the position selected by each observer is the correct one or not. Thouless found that the position at which the observers judged the retinal size of the nearer object as equal to that of the further was usually too close. They judged the retinal sizes of the two objects equal when the retinal size of the further disc was smaller.

Here we have a 'compromise' result which fits in very well with the framework analysis. Most observers were unable to make a correct retinal judgement and tended to overestimate the retinal size of the further object. Yet they never completely reverted to objective judgements. This result could very easily be explained in terms of their trying to disregard framework cues but not completely succeeding, and this explanation is entirely consistent with Rock and Ebenholtz's discovery that people cannot manage to discard framework relationships completely even when they are asked to.

So Thouless's results and the results of most other retinal size constancy experiments are consistent with the framework explanation. However, it should be pointed out that this way of explaining these constancy experiments is rather unusual. Most psychologists have adopted alternative explanations which are rather like the one produced by Thouless himself.

Thouless's analysis was in absolute terms and ignored the possible effects of framework cues. He argued that when someone sees the same object from different distances his perceptual impression of its size changes but does not change as much as does the retinal image. Somewhere between the retinal image and the perceived size the person makes an unconscious adjustment, and to this adjustment Thouless gave the name 'phenomenal regression to the real object'. He wrote 'The tendency to constancy is shown by the amount of change being a compromise between the changing size of the peripheral stimulus and the unchanging size of the real object.'

One trouble with this analysis is that it leaves quite open how it is that the observer works out what is the 'real size' of the object. Another trouble is that since it is the person's perception which is adjusted towards this 'real size' the argument implies that there is a 'real' perceptual size, that is to say a perceptual impression of an object's size which is really representative of this size. This in turn implies that there is a privileged distance between the observer and the object at which the observer gets exactly the right perceptual impression of the object's size. But what is this real perceptual size? And what is this privileged distance? There are no answers to these questions in Thouless's analysis or in subsequent discussions which have taken the same view as his.

There is therefore no pressing reason to reject the framework analysis of the results of the retinal size constancy experiments. There is, however, one awkward point for this analysis, a recent statement by Rock (1970) that the framework effects found by him and Ebenholtz do not explain constancy sufficiently. He argues that these framework effects are not great enough to explain 'the constancy which typically prevails in daily life'. But this surely is an analogy with the wrong kind of constancy. Rock is talking here about the constancy that is involved when people are judging objective sizes not retinal sizes. When people make judgements about size 'in daily life' they are concerned with the objective size of things and not with their retinal size, and this means that they will almost certainly consciously and voluntarily use other cues as well as retinal sizes. If they use framework cues, as I am suggesting they do when they can, they will do their best to incorporate these cues. If, on the other hand, they are asked to ignore these framework cues, they will try to but not succeed completely.

Three main points have emerged from this discussion. The first is that adults as well as children seem to depend very heavily on a relative code when they judge size. Secondly, adults have a strong tendency to use framework relations when they compare sizes. Thirdly, it is possible that this use of the framework is the usual basis for constancy. People probably realize that objects' sizes are constant because the relationship with their surrounds are also constant.

These points are all speculative. We need more experiments. In particular it would be interesting to know more about how children react in framework experiments and in retinal constancy experiments. There is a practical difficulty in asking children to make retinal comparisons, which is that it is very difficult to get the meaning of the task across in words to a young child, as Piaget (1969) has noted. Perhaps some non-verbal version of the task could be devised.

7
Number

Number is a continuum, and undoubtedly an extremely important one in the child's growing understanding of his environment. Number is important because it is central to so much of a typical adult's understanding – an essential ingredient, for example, in his grasp of such basic notions as time, distance, speed and quantity. An adult uses number when he measures, when he plans his behaviour, when he makes predictions. We must, therefore, discover how the young child develops his ideas about number and what effect these ideas have on his behaviour.

In some ways number is different from continua such as orientation, position and size because these are perceptual continua and number is not. A group of beads can be put on a table in several different ways. Its perceptual appearance differs and yet its number is always the same. Yet number is also a continuum and therefore raises many of the same sorts of questions. It involves relations like 'more' and 'less', and it also involves identifiable absolute points along the continuum. The relationship between 1 and 2 is the same as that between 4 and 8, and yet each of these four numbers represents a different point along the continuum. Obviously when a child learns to count and to use numbers properly he will be able to identify these four points, and he will therefore have acquired some effective internal categories which constitute an absolute code for number. But what about the child who has not yet learned how to count? Does he have any systematic way of taking in information about the number of objects in a group, and if he does, does he do so on an absolute or on a relative basis?

We have known for a long time that young children are aware of number differences and can respond to them long before they know how to count. One of the first people to make this point was Alfred Binet (1890) who was a gifted and versatile experimental psychologist as well as being a pioneer of the intelligence test. In an extremely important though little known paper he wrote: 'Before knowing how to count a child accustoms himself to the idea of numbers. He knows what it is to have many marbles or very few of them. He, therefore, makes use of an instinctive and probably unconscious numbering system before becoming acquainted with verbal numbering which we are charged with teaching him. Authors have made many interesting observations on this subject. Preyer reports some of them. He speaks of a ten-month-old child from whom it was impossible to take away one of his nine pins without his being aware of it. At eighteen months he knew perfectly well whether he was missing one of his ten animals. The question of instinctive numeration deserves careful examination through methodical experiments.' (Binet, 1890. Translated version in Pollack and Brenner, 1969).

If the young child does have systematic strategies for dealing with number, as Binet is suggesting, then we need to know what form these strategies take, how effective they are, and also how they influence the way the child eventually manages to learn how to count and to use numbers in much the same way as an adult does. In this chapter I shall argue that the basic code which the young child adopts for number is initially a relative one, and therefore that there are direct connexions between the way a child deals with number and the way he deals with perceptual continua. However, I shall also argue that for various reasons the relative number code adopted by young children is particularly inaccurate and misleading. It may be at least partly because of the weakness of the relative number code that the children begin to acquire absolute number categories relatively early on in life.

Absolute and relative number codes

By now the reader must be very familiar with the absolute-relative question. When it is applied to number the question takes the following form. What happens when a child sees two groups of objects, and when there is a different number of objects in each group? If he is aware of this difference in number, is he aware of it in a relative or in an absolute manner? Using a relative code, he could note only that one group of objects had more than the other, without taking in anything about the actual numbers involved. If, on the other hand, he used an absolute code, he would notice not only the two numbers were different, but also what the actual numbers were. This is obviously one of the first questions one should ask about the way in which young children deal with number differences, and luckily the evidence here, though remarkably sparse, is nevertheless fairly conclusive. It seems that young children initially adopt a relative code for number.

The first comprehensive evidence to show that children find it easier to note whether one of two groups is more or less numerous than to register the actual numbers involved came from a series of experiments conducted by Wohlwill (1960, 1963). His basic method was to use discrimination learning tasks with numbers in very much the same way as we did with sizes (Lawrenson and Bryant, 1972; see Chap. 2). Wohlwill's experiments also directly compared children who had to learn a relative task with children who were given an absolute task. The results of these experiments showed very clearly that relative problems tend to be easier than absolute ones.

The most comprehensive of the experiments in this series (1962) involved children aged six, eight, eleven and thirteen. All were made to learn a number discrimination task, involving a choice between two cards. Some were given pairs of cards showing only the symbols for numbers, e.g. 3, 7, and others were given pairs of cards with different numbers of figures on them. Of this second group, some (the absolute group) had to learn to respond to a particular number, 5. The rest (the relative group) had to learn to choose either the card with more or the card with fewer figures. One of the cards invariably contained 5 figures, the other 1, 2, 3, 8, or 9. Thus in half the cases the card with 5 figures was the right choice, and in the other half it was not.

The children learned the relative task much more rapidly than the absolute one in all four age groups. The superiority of the children who were given the relative task over those who were given the absolute one was also consistent over different versions of these tasks. Wohlwill tried out two different types of display, in one of which the figures on the two cards were just dots arranged in a random fashion, and in the other of which the shapes on each card were different, so that in one trial one card would contain, for example, two crosses and the other five triangles. In this type of display the figures were not arranged randomly but were set out in a straight horizontal line on each card. In both these versions of the experiment the relative problem was the easier of the two, and so it seems that children find it easier to remember relations like 'more' and 'less' than to take in and remember absolute numbers.

However, one should treat this preliminary conclusion with some caution before finally deciding that relative number codes are primary and that absolute codes are secondary and only acquired through education. There are two reasons for hesitating. The first, which is probably unimportant, concerns the distance effect, which was discussed at some length in Chapter 2. After the structures of absolute theorists like Spence and Kuenne, anyone who wants to demonstrate a relative code ought to try to demonstrate it not only with pairs which are near to each other along the continuum (near pairs) but also with pairs which are quite some way removed from each other (far pairs). One has to show that the child can learn to respond to the larger number not only when the pairs involved are, for example, 1 vs 5 and 5 vs 9, but also when quite different numbers are involved in the two pairs. So if the child is only using a relative code he should be able to learn equally well to respond to the larger number when one pair is 1 vs 5 and the other 21 vs 25. This sort of precaution is desirable because of the history of the distance effect. However, its omission is certainly not disastrous because, as we have seen, the distance effect does not really indicate the presence of an absolute code. The thing to note here is that Wohlwill's pairs are all 'near' pairs, since they all included the number 5. He had no 'far' discrimination which involved different pairs with no absolute numbers in common.

The second reason for caution is more serious. It is the age of the children, who were really quite old. They were all at school and would all have been taught something about number. It is practically certain that the three older groups knew how to count pretty well. There is, moreover, some empirical support for this suggestion because Wohlwill also found that when some other children were given a symbolic form of the absolute and relative tasks, with actual number symbols on the cards instead of different numbers of dots, the older children learned the absolute task more easily than the relative task. All these children therefore had been trained in number and many had actually learned a lot about it. Thus it is possible that they use relative codes with some ease only because they have been taught to. After all, learning about number does not only involve picking up an absolute code. Children also begin to deal with number relations quite systematically when, for example, they are taught how to divide.

This means we cannot conclude from this experiment that relative codes occur earlier in development, and the crucial question is still the one raised originally by Binet. How does the child deal with number differences when he has not yet been taught to count? Is he aware of these differences, and if he is, what form does his awareness take?

Recently (Bryant, 1972a) reported an experiment with four-year-old children, none of whom could count beyond 10. This experiment involved a direct comparison between absolute and relative groups, and was thus very similar to Wohlwill's study. However, our experiment included a 'far' relative task as well as a 'near' one.

This experiment involved four different pairs of numbers: 10 vs 12, 12 vs 14, 20 vs 22 and 22 vs 24. Every child learned a discrimination which involved two of these pairs and he was given one of these pairs on half the trials and the other on the other half. The children in the absolute group were either given the 10/12 and the 12/14 pairs in which case they had to learn always to pick the card with 12 figures, or they were given the 20/22 and 22/24 pairs and had to learn to pick the card with 22 figures on it. The near relative group was also given these combinations of pairs but they had in each case to learn to respond either always to the larger number or to the smaller one. The far relative group however were given the two extreme pairs 10/12 and 22/24, and they too had to learn to respond either to the larger or smaller number. Thus the experiment was with children younger than Wohlwill's and included a 'far' control.

The results were on the whole very clear. The young children had little difficulty with the relative task. On the other hand, the absolute tasks were very hard and were usually not learned by these four-year-olds. Thus we can extend Wohlwill's original conclusion. It seems to apply also to younger children who cannot count much. These children also primarily use a relative code for number.

One further point about these results is interesting. There was no difference between the children in the relative group who had to learn to choose the card with 'more' and those who had to choose the one with 'less'. Both types of relations were equally easy. This is interesting because some very ingenious work by Donaldson and Balfour (1968) on children's understanding of relative terms has shown that children of around this age level usually understand the meaning of the word 'more' much better than that of 'less'. Many children responded to the word 'more' correctly, and yet reacted to the word 'less' as though it also meant more.

Donaldson and Balfour's task was a verbal one and ours was not. The fact that the difficulty with 'less' occurred in their task and not in ours suggests that young children have no difficulty with handling and remembering the relation 'less'. Their difficulty is a linguistic one.

Two major implications follow from the conclusion that the primary code which children adopt for number differences is a relative one. The first is that there is a very obvious connexion between the way children deal with number and the way they deal with perceptual information about their environment. We now have very good evidence that young children adopt very much the same relative strategy with number, and the interesting point is that this strategy is bound to lead the child into the same sorts of difficulties with number as with orientation, position and size. Once again we can note that the limitation of a relative code is that it does not tell the child anything about the actual number in a particular group of objects, in exactly the same way as a relative orientation code does not allow him to take in the actual orientation of a specific object.

The next question to ask is how the child gets round the limitations of a relative number code, and this leads us to the second main implication, which is that with numbers there is no simple way round. The child's perceptual frame of reference often allows him to make perceptual inferences about continua like orientation and these inferences help him get over the weaknesses of a code based only on relations. A single line, particularly a horizontal or a vertical line, will often parallel some of the features of its background. But what is there in the background which will provide a similar 'match' signal for number? Suppose that I set out ten marbles on the carpet, take them away, and then replace them, asking the child whether their number is now the same as it was before. There is normally nothing in the background of the carpet which will help him tell whether the number has changed or not, unless the marbles fall into exactly the same spots as before and these spots are distinguishable from others, which is most unlikely. On the other hand, if I put a pencil on the carpet, remove it and then replace it, asking the child whether its orientation is now the same as it was the first time, the carpet will probably provide suitable framework cues for a perceptual inference. If the pencil was originally parallel to one of the carpet's sides or to a line on the carpet, it will still be parallel if it is replaced in the same orientation, even if its position on the carpet is now different. In much the same way most other frameworks would be more suitable for perceptual continua like orientation than for number. It is quite probable of course that young children can make deductive inferences about number as well as about other continua. The only trouble is that the usual frame of reference does not permit him to use these inferences as a way of remembering something about the number of objects in a particular group.

It follows from this analysis that the young child's codes for number are initially a great deal less effective than his equivalent codes for perceptual continua. Moreover, the inefficiency of the way in which he deals with number is made even more striking by the discovery that some of the cues which he uses to make relative judgments about number are quite wrong. As a result, his immediate relative judgements can often be totally incorrect.

Correct and incorrect cues for judgements about number

In the 1890 paper mentioned above, Binet also suggested that the strategies which young children used to judge number, though systematic, were often wrong. He wrote: 'In the little children under our observation the perception and comparisons of lengths occurred with remarkable correctness; on the other hand the perception of numbers was often extremely gross and defective' (Binet, 1890).

Binet's evidence for the 'grossness' of children's judgements of number was derived mainly from an experiment in which he asked a four-year-old girl to compare two parallel rows of counters and to say which of the two rows had more counters in it. One row contained 16 large counters, the other 18 small ones. Because the larger counters took up more space, their row was actually the longer despite the fact that it contained less counters.

Binet found that the young child quite consistently got this comparison wrong, judging that the longer, but less numerous, row had the greater number of counters. Even when the number of counters in the less numerous row was reduced still further, the child again maintained that this row had more counters as long as it took up more physical space than the other row.

Note that the child was not acting randomly: she was using a cue quite consistently, but it was the wrong cue. The amount of space taken up by a particular row of counters is fairly independent of the number of counters in it. That young children are influenced by the length cue when they judge number has been amply confirmed by many people since then. Piaget (1968) has shown that they often judge number on the basis of the length of the rows that have to be compared, and many other people as well have demonstrated that young children are very strongly influenced by the length cue. Gelman (1972) has written an excellent review of the literature on children's number judgements, which collects a formidable body of evidence showing young children's peculiar leaning towards this incorrect cue.

It is fairly worrying to find that the young child will quite consistently say that the longer of two rows is the more numerous even when it is not, because it may mean that the child and the experimenter are misunderstanding each other. It may be that the child who is asked to pick the row with 'more' thinks that he is being asked not about number but about length and chooses the row with more length because that is what he thinks he has to do. However there are two good reasons for thinking that the child does understand that the question is about number and that he genuinely thinks that length is a relevant cue for number judgements. The first is that in other displays the child uses other, but correct, cues when he is asked to make a number comparison. The second is that he uses correct and incorrect cues for number interchangeably and treats them as equivalent.

The first point is very simple. The best example of an effective cue used by young children who cannot count correctly is the so–called 'one-to-one correspondence cue', when, for instance, two rows are placed alongside one another like two ranks of soldiers and the child is given the chance to check each member of each row with its obvious counterpart in the opposite row. As we have seen, young children can use such in-line cues very easily. A glance at the two A displays in Fig. 7.1 shows how this one-to-one correspondence could work.

It was mainly Piaget who first drew attention to the possible importance of this cue, and there is now very good evidence that young children do use it as a basis for number judgements long before they can count. For example, we gave the three types of display in Fig. 7.1 to children aged from three to six years in a recent experiment (Bryant, 1972b) and their performance showed quite clearly that they use the one-to-one correspondence cue as consistently as they use the length cue. In the two A displays, which can be solved on the basis of one-to-one correspondence, the children were quite consistently correct – as consistently correct, in fact, as they were consistently incorrect in the B comparisons in which length was the main cue. In the third display C in which neither the one-to-one correspondence cue nor the length cue were available the young children tended to make quite random choices. It seems, then, first that the child's ability to make a consistent choice depends very much on what display he is given and, secondly, that when he does make a consistent choice, he sometimes uses cues

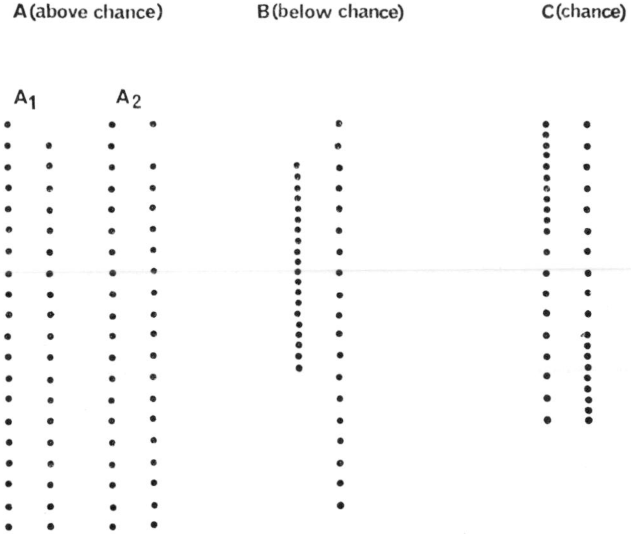

Figure 7.1

which are correct and sometimes cues which are incorrect, again depending on the display which he is given. The same child who uses the incorrect length cue will also at other times use the correct one-to-one correspondence cue.

The one-to-one correspondence cue has two important features to it. The first is that, as I have already noted, it is a correct cue. The second feature is that the one-to-one correspondence cue is *par excellence* a relative cue. If the child simply cancels out object against object until all the objects in the less numerous row are accounted for, and one or more objects remain unaccounted for in the more numerous row, he can only say which row has more: he is not in a position to say what absolute numbers are involved. This point is an extremely important one, because it is often maintained that young children are not really responding to number differences until they know their numbers. This is quite wrong. When the child who cannot count uses the one-to-one correspondence cue he is responding to a number difference consistently and correctly, but he is responding in a relative way. The fact that children use this cue before they count is a very clear indication that the development is likely to be from relative to absolute codes.

It could be argued that although children use the one-to-one correspondence cue, it is in real life a relatively trivial cue because it is man-made. The argument would be that things are not naturally laid out in an orderly one-to-one manner, unless they have been artificially arranged that way by man. However, this would seem to be an undeserved slight upon the importance of this very pervasive cue. After all we are dealing not with man in the wild but with children who live in a man-made environment, and whose world is full of displays which can very convincingly be described as organized in a one-to-one correspondence manner. He sees two rows of identical houses arranged opposite each other in a one-to-one fashion, and he walks through rows of trees planted in this way as well. He looks through windows whose different panes are arranged in an orderly one-to-one manner, and sees bricks on the outsides of houses and books on bookshelves and eggs in boxes and floor tiles inside the house. In all these displays rows of discrete objects are laid alongside one another in a one-to-one manner. The arrangements are man-made, but they are all around the child.

It could, however, be argued that the one-to-one correspondence cue does not work in the way I have suggested, and that children are not cancelling out object by object but are simply using a 'density' cue. Gelman (unpublished) has pointed out that rows with different numbers will differ either in length or in density, so that if one makes length equal the child who gets it right is using the other cue. For example, they would solve the problem in display A_2 (Fig. 7.1) by going to the row of greater average density. However, there is now some clear evidence that the young child does use the one-to-one correspondence cue.

In the absolute-relative experiment which was described in the last section (Bryant, 1972a) the displays used were A-type, one-to-one correspondence displays. This experiment also included a post-test which was given to the children who had learned the relative task. The post-test lasted for ten trials and in it children were given sometimes A-type displays and sometimes B-type displays. Suppose now that the child who had been trained to respond to the row with 'more' was given these displays. If he learned to solve the original problem by choosing the denser of the two displays, he should in the post-test continue to respond to the numerous row in the A-type displays and he should also respond to the more numerous row in the B-type displays since in these displays the more numerous row is also the denser one. On the other hand, if, as I am arguing, he solves the original problem on a one-to-one correspondence basis and he thinks that both this and length are genuine cues for length, he should in the post-test continue to be right in the A-type displays and yet actually make the wrong response to the longer, less numerous (and less dense) row in the post-test. This is actually what happened. The children tended to continue to be right with the A-type displays and yet to be consistently wrong with the B-type displays. They were plainly not using the density cue all the time, since if they responded to the denser row in one type of display they chose the less dense cue in the other, and vice versa.

We can conclude two things. The first is that children do genuinely use the one-to-one correspondence cue and that they use it and not density to solve the A-type display. The second, very interesting, conclusion is that they use the length and the one-to-one correspondence cue interchangeably. Having learned to go to the row with more counters on the basis of the one-to-one correspondence cue they then go to the longer row in a display in which the two rows have different lengths even when the longer row is the less numerous one. It seems that as far as young children are concerned both cues are equally good. They think, quite wrongly, that the two cues will produce the same result.

We can conclude, then, not only that young children use relative cues as a basis for their judgements about number, but also that they consistently use at least two different sets of relative cues. It follows that there are two ways in which the child's judgements about numbers are 'gross and defective'. First, these judgements are relative but usually cannot be bolstered by framework cues in the way that relative judgements about perceptual continua can. Secondly, some of the cues which children use to make these judgements about numbers are incorrect, which means that the judgements themselves will often be quite inaccurate.

We have to ask how the child eventually manages to get round these grave difficulties. The obvious answer is that he learns to count and thus acquires an absolute code, which avoids many of the difficulties of a relative code and is certainly superior to a relative code which is often going to be wrong. This is probably also the correct explanation. However, as we shall see, it is not a simple, all or nothing development. Young children seem to acquire an absolute code for some numbers, small numbers, earlier than for other numbers, and long before they get any formal training about numbers at school.

Small vs large numbers

Although it is almost certainly true that the young child's primary code for number differences is relative, there is also some very good evidence that from a very early age he has an absolute code for some numbers, and these tend to be small numbers like one, two and three. This discrepancy between small and large numbers, which was once very neatly described by Descoeudres (1921) as the 'un, deux, trois, beaucoup' phenomenon, has been noticed by many psychologists who work with young children.

The first person to provide any comprehensive empirical evidence for a difference in the way young children coped with small and large numbers was again Binet (1890) in the same important paper on children's reactions to number and to length. Binet noticed that when children were given rows to compare in which the counters were 'spaced irregularly' they made fewer successful comparisons when numbers as large as 21 and 22 were involved than they did with smaller numbers.

Then in the 1920s two large scale pieces of work (Descoeudres, 1921; Beckman, 1924) confirmed that children have very much less difficulty with small than with large number comparisons and these studies also showed that this was because young children seem to have an absolute code which permits them to recognize small numbers up to about 5. The basic task which was given to the two- to six-year-old children in Descoeudres' study was to watch the experimenter laying out a certain number of objects, and then to lay out the same number of objects themselves in an exactly similar group. She found that children between two and four years can manage to do this when two or three objects are involved but then make many errors with large numbers. Beckman also produced very much the same result in a study that was very similar to Descoeudres', except for the fact that Beckman actually said what the numbers were to the children he tested, whereas Descoeudres never mentioned any numbers at all.

These early results suggest that children do have some absolute code for small numbers with which they can replace their more unreliable relative codes. A very recent experiment by Gelman (1972) not only confirms this conclusion but provides a direct contrast between situations in which children use an absolute number code and situations in which they use the incorrect relative cue for length. Gelman's procedure was very simple. She showed four- and five-year-old children 'triads' of numbers of figures, and asked them to show her which two had the same number. Of three figures A, B, and C, note that two (A and B) might have the same number of dots and two (A and C) might have the same length. So if the child says that A and C have the same number of dots he is using the length cue while if he chooses A and B he is probably responding to the actual number of dots involved, since the other main cue, one-to-one correspondence, is not available here. Gelman's procedure was fairly complex in that it involved many triads and many different numbers. However, her results were very clear indeed. The four- and five-year-old children nearly always made their choice correctly on the basis of numbers when the number of the dots involved were 2 and 3. However, with larger numbers they made more errors and the larger the numbers involved the more errors they made. Moreover, when they did not respond on the basis of number, the cue which they nearly always chose was length. On the other hand, the amount of dots involved did not seem to have any effect on an older seven-year-old group of children. Here is a clear sign that young children use different codes for different numbers. They use an absolute code, and a correct one, for small numbers, and a relative length code, which is incorrect, for larger numbers.

Two points can be made about this result. The first is that it raises the question of how young children develop an absolute code for small numbers so early. One intriguing possibility is that it has something to do with the process which has come to be known as subitizing (Woodworth and Schlosberg, 1954, Chap. 4; Neisser, 1967). The term 'subitizing' refers to some evidence that adults appear to be able to estimate a small number of items without having to count them. With larger numbers, above about 7 or 8 items, they have to count. Some people (Klahr and Wallace, 1973: Wallace, 1972) have tried to suggest that children initially build up absolute codes for smaller numbers not by learning to count but purely on a perceptual basis. This is an interesting suggestion, but it is probably wrong because, as Beckman (1924) pointed out some time ago, young children seem only to manage to recognize smaller numbers after they have learned to count as far as the numbers involved. Beckman showed, for example, that it is only after children can count to 3 that they can manage to recognize the absolute number of objects in a group of 3: Beckman's argument that counting precedes subitizing and not the other way round, certainly seems a convincing one.

The second point is a more relevant one to the main argument of this book. Gelman's experiment together with the work of Descoeudres and Beckman demonstrates the presence of an absolute code, albeit an extremely limited one, in very young children. It seems very likely that they begin to acquire an effective absolute code for number before they do so for any of the other continua which have been mentioned in other chapters. This need not surprise us however because the relative codes which children use for other continua are probably very much more effective than their relative codes for number.

Certainly, it is very likely that a child who uses both the one-to-one correspondence cue and the length cue, will not only make relative judgements which are wrong but, more seriously for him, will make relative judgements about the same groups of objects which are completely inconsistent with one another. Suppose, for example, that a child sees two rows of counters, one longer than the other, and judges that the longer row has more: then the shorter row is stretched out till it is even longer than the originally longer one. What is the child to think? He can see that nothing has been added or taken away, and yet his first judgement is that one row is more numerous and his second is that the other one is. Obviously, if the child uses length as a cue for number he will be in trouble when the length of a row of objects is changed. Thus the very fact that young children definitely do use this cue makes it necessary for us to consider not just the question of the way children compare the number of two static groups of objects but also how they react when the perceptual appearances of individual groups of objects are changed. The next chapter will deal with this second problem.

This leaves unanswered one intriguing question about the young child's relative codes for number. Why does he use the length cue so consistently and with such persistence? There is as yet no glimmer of a clue as to why he chooses this misleading cue. Yet the answer to this question might have considerable educational as well as theoretical significance. Obviously, the child must abandon the length cue if he is to acquire an effective understanding of number. If we know why he takes up this cue in the first place we shall be in a better position to show him that it is quite inappropriate.

Relative number codes, cardination, and ordination

Adults use numbers in both a cardinal and an ordinal sense. They know that when the number of objects in two groups of objects is the same there will be a one-to-one correspondence between the two groups, so that each member of each group will be matched by another member in the other group. This is the cardinal sense. The ordinal sense refers to the ordering of different numbers, and to the knowledge that 2 is greater than 1, 3 greater than 2 and 1, and so on.

To what extent is the young child, who cannot count properly and still depends primarily on relative codes, able to cope with the cardinal and ordinal aspects of number? If my hypothesis is correct, the child's relative codes should in some ways be suitable for cardinal and for ordinal judgements and in other ways quite unsuitable. Let us take first of all the cardinal aspect. We have seen that children are able to use one-to-one correspondence as a cue. However, they can only do so in restricted circumstances. The one-to-one correspondence has to be spatial in nature. The children have to be able to use the in-line cue to judge whether or not each member of one group is matched by its counterpart. If the two groups of objects are not matched up in the military style, which is the characteristic of displays A_1 and A_2 in Fig. 7.1, the child cannot use one-to-one correspondence to make his judgement about the relative numbers in the two groups. He cannot work out which of the two rows in display C in Fig. 7.1 is the more numerous.

In the case of ordinal numbers, too, the child should be able to understand some things but not others. We have seen (Chap. 3) that children as young as four are able to make transitive deductive inferences about length and there is no reason for thinking that they could not also make similar inferences about number. To be able to make a transitive inference is to be able to put things in an ordinal relationship. If the child works out $A > C$ from the information that $A > B$ and that $B > C$ then he must understand the $A > B > C$ order. To this extent he must understand ordinal relationships. However, his ability to cope with these relationships will on the whole be rather limited. As we have seen the young child often fails to make transitive inferences and therefore to put things in order, because he does not remember the direct information which he has to co-ordinate in order to make the inference. If he does not remember that $A > B$ or that $B > C$ he cannot possibly put them in the correct order.

Thus the relative to absolute development, which, I am arguing, is the crucial change in the young child's dealings with number, cuts right across the cardinal–ordinal distinction. If my argument is right, there would be no sense in asking whether the child develops an understanding of cardinal number before ordinal number or vice versa. However, there has been at least one attempt to suggest that one of these aspects of number precedes the other in the young child's development. This was made by Brainerd (1973).

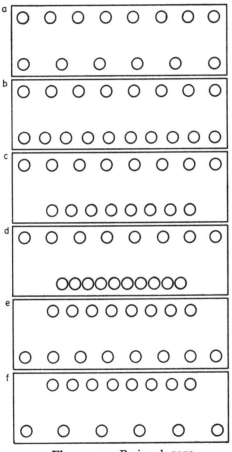

Figure 7.2 Brainerd, 1973

Brainerd suggested that the child understands ordinal number before cardinal number. He worked with children aged between five and seven years. His cardinal test was exactly the same as the traditional transitivity experiment. In one ordinal test he gave children three clay balls, whose sizes were the same, but whose weights were different.

The child was asked to compare the heaviest with the medium weight in one direct comparison and the medium with the lightest in another. Having done this the child was asked about the relationship between the two weights (the lightest and the heaviest) which he had not compared directly. In the other ordinal test he showed the children rods of different lengths, but otherwise his procedure was exactly the same. Brainerd's argument was that if children understand ordinal relationships they should be able to make the transitive inference in both the weight and the length problems.

Brainerd's cardinal tests involved comparisons between two parallel rows of circles. The children were shown six displays. Brainerd's aim was to see whether the children could recognize one-to-one correspondence or not. The six displays are reproduced in Fig. 7.2 which shows that in some cases the number of figures in each row is the same while in others it is different. None of the six displays is arranged in an in-line way. This means that there is no spatial one-to-one correspondence cue to show when the different rows match exactly and when they do not.

Brainerd found that there were children who made errors in both the ordinal and the cardinal tasks. However, he also found that the ordinal tasks were far the easier. Nearly all the children who could manage the cardinal task could also manage the ordinal one, whereas 87 per cent of the children who could solve the ordinal task perfectly well could not yet answer the cardinal questions properly. He concluded that the understanding of cardinal number precedes that of ordinal number in the child's development.

The trouble with this conclusion is that Brainerd's tests were in many ways quite wrong for young children. His ordinal tests suffered all the faults of the traditional transitivity test because they involved memory. Moreover, in the cardinal tests the one-to-one correspondence was not reflected in the row's spatial arrangements, and this omission no doubt explains the peculiar difficulty of these cardinal tests.

So Brainerd's results can be explained in terms of the child's dependence on relative codes which themselves are very heavily influenced by the perceptual display. The reason that children were so bad at spotting one-to-one correspondence in his cardinal test was simply that the displays were not suited to the children's relative codes.

We can conclude that as far as the child's development is concerned the cardinal–ordinal distinction is not particularly important. What is significant is the way in which the child abandons his relative strategies

and acquires an effective absolute code for number. We can now turn
to the question of how, before he acquires such an absolute code, his
inadequate and contradictory relative codes affect his response to
changes in the perceptual appearance of a group of objects.

8

Invariance

The number in a group of objects stays the same even when the perceptual appearance of the group changes so long as nothing is added and nothing taken away. If the child is to learn how to use number properly he must get to know about this sort of invariance.

Yet some of the evidence which was discussed in the last chapter implies that young children might have very great difficulty with this invariance principle. We have seen that children often use quite inappropriate cues, such as length, as a basis for judgements about number. Suppose that the child who uses length is shown a row of objects. He sees it transformed perceptually by being spread out. Will he not think that the number of objects in the row has increased? The question is obviously an important one because unless the child does understand the invariance principle there is very little that he will be able to understand about number. If he does not understand that a group of six objects remains a group of six objects unless something is added or taken away he does not really understand what 'six' means.

This is an extremely familiar question. The first person to consider it systematically was Piaget (1952). As we have seen, one of Piaget's main ideas about the child younger than roughly seven or eight years is that he is dominated by his immediate perceptual input, which he is unable to reorganise once it arrives. Not surprisingly Piaget was attracted to the idea that perceptually dominated children might treat a perceptual transformation of a group of objects as a real change in their number. If this idea were correct it would mean that the child would have no understanding of the invariance principle.

At first sight it must seem that this hypothesis of Piaget's is an extremely plausible one. After all if a young child does consistently use the length cue to compare two different rows, it seems very likely that he will also use the same cue in much the same way when he sees the length of a row of objects being transformed. Nevertheless, we need some empirical evidence.

This necessary step was taken by Piaget and his colleagues in his important and well known series of conservation experiments. The results of these were offered as evidence that young children do not understand the principle of invariance properly and that they often think that perceptual transformations constitute a real change in quantity. However, these experiments, as we shall see, are not completely convincing, and subsequent research produces a very different picture of the young child's ability to use the invariance principle.

The conservation experiment

Piaget and his colleagues called their experiments 'conservation' experiments because they were designed as tests of young children's ability to understand that rows of counters, balls of plasticine or volumes

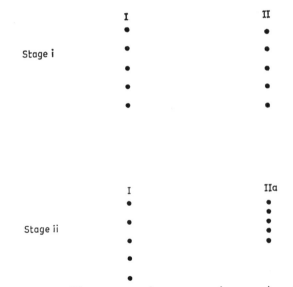

Figure 8.1 The two stages in a conservation experiment

of liquid conserve their quantity even when their perceptual appearance changes. One familiar example of the conservation experiment is given in Fig. 8.1. This is actually an experiment on the conservation of number, and I shall confine my analysis to this example.

The experiment involves two stages. In the number problem, as Fig. 8.1 demonstrates, the child is first shown two rows, I and II, and is asked whether their number is the same or not.

The two rows are arranged side by side in a one-to-one correspondence manner. They are equal in number, and they are the same length. This means that if the child uses either the one-to-one correspondence cue or the length cue or even applies some absolute code, he will judge the two rows as equal, as indeed they are. This concludes the first stage. Then the experimenter takes one of the rows, II, and bunches it up (IIa). It is now shorter than row I which has been left untouched. The experimenter asks the child for the second time whether the number of counters in each row is equal or not. The consistent result of this experiment is that children do not produce the right answer until they reach the age of roughly six or seven years. Younger than this they answer correctly only in the first stage. This was Piaget's original discovery and it has been confirmed many times since he first made it (Elkind, 1964; Dodwell, 1962).

Piaget reached two conclusions from these results. The first concerns the older children who got the problem right. He argued that they must understand that shortening the row did not change its number because they gave the same response after it was shortened as they did before. His second conclusion is about the younger child. He believed that the wrong response showed that the child did not properly understand the invariance of number, but treated a perceptual transformation as a real change. These are conclusions which have been very widely accepted, not only by psychologists, but also by people concerned with education and particularly with the question of how young children should be taught about number.

What is one to make of Piaget's argument? The crucial question is whether the traditional conservation experiments do demonstrate in a watertight manner that the young child does not understand invariance, and that he thinks when he sees a row of counters being spread out that the number of counters is also being changed. In the next section I shall argue that there are some serious problems about the design of the experiment, and reasons for doubting that it actually shows anything very definite about the young child's understanding of invariance.

Criticisms of the conservation experiment

There are two patterns of behaviour to be explained: the so-called 'conservation response' typical of the older child, and the 'non-conservation response' found in children under six or seven years of age. Piaget's analysis of these can, and should, be taken quite separately.

The conservation response

Piaget's conclusion about the conservation response is uncontroversial and almost certainly correct. One can be fairly certain that the older children have a working understanding of the invariance principle. But these children may arrive at their correct responses by using either an absolute or a relative code. The conservation experiment does not show which. An absolute code would tell them that the numbers in I and in IIa were the same, and also that the number in the transformed row was the same after the transformation as before.

We can take as an hypothetical alternative the child who produces the conservation response but does not reach the correct conclusion on the basis of the absolute numbers involved. This will mean that his judgement in the first stage of the experiment, that the two rows (I and II) are equal, is a relative one. He knows that these two rows are the same without having any idea how many counters there are in each row. This relative response is perfectly possible, because the two rows are originally arranged in a one-to-one correspondence manner. Then one row is transformed, and this one-to-one correspondence is thus destroyed. The child now has no relative cue to give him the correct answer. This means that if he does answer that they are equal, he must do so on the basis of information transferred from the first display. The interesting thing about this transfer is that it must be based on the invariance principle. The transfer must depend on the child reasoning first that I equals II and then that II equals IIa (which is the invariance principle) and then inferring that therefore I must equal IIa.

This is a deductive, transitive inference, and it is true that if the child is using only a relative code and manages to solve the conservation problem, he must understand invariance, and he must also be able to make a deductive inference. He must be able to combine his understanding that the quantity has remained unchanged over the perceptual transformation with his memory for his first judgement that the two quantities involved are equal, and then he must infer that they are still equal after the transformation.

We owe the insight that conservation tasks may require inferences as well as an understanding of invariance to an interesting paper written by Elkind (1967) on the conservation experiment. Elkind assumes that children only use relative codes in the conservation task and although this is probably not true, at least as far as number tasks are concerned, nevertheless his point about inferences is very valuable.

The conservation failure

Piaget's second conclusion, which concerns the children who fail in the conservation task poses much greater problems of interpretation. His suggestion is that such children believe that reorganizing the spatial arrangement of a row of counters actually changes the number of counters in it. The first thing to say is that this explanation is quite plausible. It is certainly possible that the child really thinks that spreading out a row increases its number.

The trouble is that there are at least three alternative ways of explaining failures in the conservation task. If there were anything to these alternatives one would have to say that the meaning of the errors in the conservation task was essentially ambiguous and therefore the design of the experiment weak. So we need to look quite carefully into their nature. They are that the error is caused either (1) by memory failure or (2) by a failure to make inferences or (3) by a conflict between incompatible judgements.

(1) *Memory failure*

There is the possibility that the young child who fails has simply forgotten what the first display, which he saw before the transformation, was like. We have seen that if he uses a relative code he has two pieces of information which he must combine inferentially, $I = II$ and $II = IIa$. It may be that he understands that II must equal IIa, and thus understands the invariance principle, but that he has forgotten that II in its original state was the same as I. This would mean that even though he understands that the changed row has the same number, he cannot produce the correct response after the transformation because he lacks the information for the necessary inference. There is nothing in the conservation design to rule out the possibility of this sort of failure in memory. Ideally, one would like an experiment in which the child failed to solve the task in the experimental condition and yet in a control condition could be shown to be using his memory for the original display; there is certainly nothing like this control in the conservation experiment.

However, some fairly recent evidence suggests that the memory failure is not a serious problem in these sorts of tasks. Bruner and his colleagues (Bruner *et al.*, 1966, Chap. 9) have shown that children who would normally fail conservation tasks do have some memory of the appearance of a display before a transformation. Also an experiment of ours (Bryant, 1972b), which will be described in some detail later on in this chapter, demonstrated that children who consistently err in tasks very similar to the number conservation problem nevertheless perform very well in a control condition which requires that they remember what the relations between two rows of counters were before a perceptual transformation. So although it is a serious weakness of the conservation experiment that it does not include a control for forgetting, we can conclude for the moment that children's conservation failures are not on the whole caused by lapses in memory.

(2) *Inference failure*

As we have seen, the child who uses a relative code has to make a transitive inference to solve the conservation problem. He might fail because though he could remember that I equalled II and understand that II equalled IIa (the invariance principle) he was yet unable to combine these two pieces of information to conclude that I and IIa are the same.

This point was made by Elkind (1967) when he showed that conservation problems often involve a hidden transitive inference. Elkind then went on to suggest that there were two kinds of conservation, 'conservation of identity' which means realizing the invariance of II when transformed to IIa, and 'conservation of equivalence' which involved incorporating this information into a transitive inference. Now this second suggestion is rather an odd one, because Elkind seems to be trying quite unjustifiably to convert a point about experimental design into a conceptual point.

To show that the solution to a task involves both an inference and an understanding of invariance is simply to demonstrate that the child who fails can do so for more than one reason, and therefore that the experimental design, at least as far as it concerns the interpretation of errors, is essentially ambiguous. One cannot then go on to say that this means that there are two kinds of conservation. Experiments are set up to test something, and the conservation experiment's purpose is to test whether or not the child understands invariance. Elkind's analysis shows that the traditional conservation experiment is not doing this job properly. His analysis does not show that there are two types of conservation.

Nevertheless, the argument is a good one as far as it concerns experimental design. There are two points which should be made here. The first is that it is now clear that Piaget himself has two alternative explanations for the same result. He says that young children do not understand invariance, and also that they cannot make transitive inferences. Both these incapacities would lead to errors in the conservation task.

The second point is that although the argument about inferences is a sound one it is probably not, in the end, very important because as we have seen in Chapter 3 young children can make transitive inferences. They are able to combine two separate pieces of information to reach a new conclusion and thus their errors in conservation tasks are probably not due to failures in inferences. Later on in this chapter it will be shown that the most valuable thing to come out of Elkind's analysis was that it provoked a new kind of conservation experiment, which has produced a completely different and more plausible set of conclusions about young children's reactions to perceptual transformations.

(3) Conflict between incompatible judgements

The final objection to the invariance explanation of failures in the conservation experiment is a relatively new one, but is probably the most serious of the three. To appreciate its importance one has to put oneself in the young child's shoes. Remember that the child uses sometimes the length cue and sometimes the one-to-one correspondence cue to judge the relative number of two simultaneously presented rows of objects, and that he uses the incorrect length cue as consistently as he uses the correct one-to-one correspondence cue. This must mean that as far as the child is concerned these two cues are as good as each other. He does not know which is the better.

Now look again at the traditional conservation procedure in Fig. 8.1. It involves showing the child first a display which on the basis of one-to-one correspondence produces one judgement and then converting it into a second display which, on the basis of the length cue, would normally produce a completely different judgement. The first of these displays presented on its own normally produces the judgement that the rows are equal: the second display presented on its own would normally produce the judgement that the rows are unequal. As far as the child is concerned these two judgements are as good and as firmly based as each other. He has no way of knowing that the first is better than the second. Therefore when the first display is transformed into the second in the traditional procedure, why should he maintain the first judgement against the second? Obviously, the judgements produced by the first and the second display conflict, but the young child has absolutely no systematic way of resolving this conflict.

It follows that the child who says first that the rows are equal and then after the transformation that they are not does not necessarily think that the rows have changed in number. He may understand that a perceptual transformation does not actually change numbers, but still be unable to solve this conflict between two opposite judgements. In fact, the only thing which we can be certain about is that he definitely will be faced with this conflict and will surely have no way of resolving it. Whether he also thinks that the numbers are altered by a spatial transformation is another matter. Gelman (1972) has given us a very apposite and amusing allegory which takes the form of a story about a duck hunter (an adult) watching a flock of wild ducks and wondering how many there are in the flock. First, while they are all in the air he judges that there are 150 of them: later when they all settle on a lake he changes his mind and judges instead that there are about 75. He knows that these are the same ducks and that there have been no additions to the group or desertions from it. However, his judgement about their number has changed because of a perceptual transformation. The point of this story is that the man alters his judgement after the transformation, and yet does not believe that the actual number of the ducks has changed. He knows instead that one of his two judgements is wrong and on the whole accepts the more recent of the two.

This story is not the exact analogy of the young child's dilemma in the conservation task, because Gelman's hunter is using absolute codes about the number of a single group, while the young child is almost certainly dealing with the relative values of two groups. However, apart from this difference the story is an excellent illustration of the young child's basic difficulties in the conservation task.

The force of this alternative explanation of the non-conservation response lies in the fact that the child must undergo this sort of conflict in the conservation problem whether or not he understands the invariance principle. The very fact that he ordinarily uses the length cue quite consistently shows both that he thinks that this cue is a correct one and that he does not realize that it is any less correct than the one-to-one correspondence cue. This must mean that the conservation problem faces him with a conflict which he can resolve only by the arbitrary method of favouring the judgement which is prompted by the more recent display.

Again there is no control for this alternative explanation in the traditional conservation procedure, and since the objection is rather a serious one it follows that the usual conservation design is weak. We need some different experiments designed in a way that allows a distinction between errors which are due to the sort of conflict just described, and errors which quite definitely show that the child who makes them does not understand the principle of invariance.

Most of the work with the conservation problem has been carried out within the framework of Piaget's hypothesis about invariance. Perhaps then a better way of sorting out the relative merits of these two alternative explanations is to look more closely at the hypothesis about conflict, and to see what predictions it makes.

The conflict hypothesis produces two main predictions. The first is that once conflict has been removed the child should be able to apply the principle of invariance very effectively. The second is that showing the child that one of the two judgements which he makes in the conservation situation is soundly based and the other is not, should resolve his conflict and make it possible for him to answer the conservation problem correctly. We can consider these two predictions, and the evidence on them, separately.

Removing conflict

So far in this chapter we have considered only displays with which children make quite consistent judgements. Yet there are also other displays with which children are quite at sea, and behave completely randomly. These chance-level displays are actually another very good piece of evidence that young children use relative rather than absolute codes to make judgements about number. These displays could be solved by an absolute code but do not offer the cues which children usually use to make relative number judgements.

The three displays (Fig. 8.2) A, B, and C, which we have already encountered in Chapter 7, are a very good example of how children make consistent judgements about number with some displays but not with others. In each display one row contains 19 the other 20 counters.

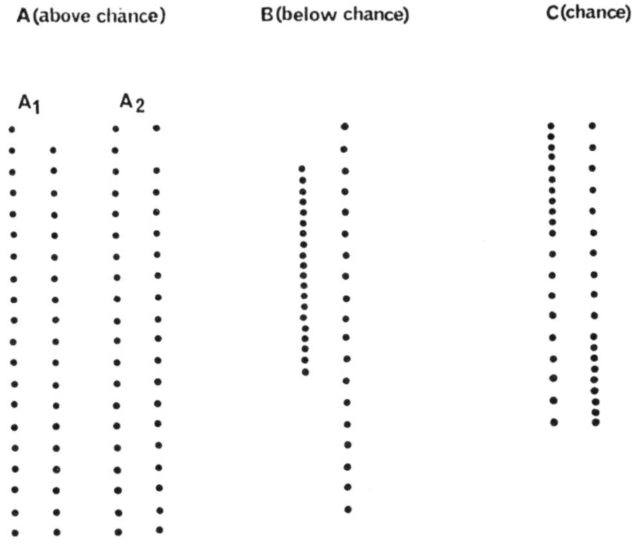

A (above chance)   B (below chance)   C (chance)

Figure 8.2

A is the above-chance-level display and B the below-chance-level display in that young children are consistently correct with A and consistently incorrect with B. However, with the C display young children are at chance-level (Bryant, 1972): when they are asked which of the two rows has more counters the children choose the correct and the incorrect row equally often. The reason for this random behaviour is obvious. The display does not allow the children to use either of their main relative cues. The rows are equal in length and the counters are not arranged in a one-to-one correspondence manner, and so the child has nothing to go on when he has to judge which row has more counters.

Chance-level displays are interesting in themselves but their major importance at this point of the discussion is that they offer a very convenient way of removing conflict, and yet testing whether the child uses the invariance principle. Suppose, for example, that the child was first shown one of the A displays and that this was then transformed, with the child looking on, into display C. We know that the child makes consistent and correct judgements with A, and that he does not with C, when C is presented on its own. So the interesting question is whether the child will do better with C after a transformation from A than he does with C when it is presented on its own. If his performance with C is better than chance-level after the transformation from A then he will definitely have transferred information about the relative quantities of the two rows across the perceptual transformation, and this transfer must be based on some understanding that the number of counters in each row has stayed the same. Thus the transformation tests the child's ability to use the invariance principle and yet it avoids conflict. The typical judgements which a child makes about the A and the C displays do not conflict because there is nothing in C to conflict with A, in that the child's usual behaviour with C is random. Thus the conflict hypothesis would predict that young children would transfer information across this transformation from A to C.

The main purpose of a recent experiment (Bryant 1972b, Exp. 1) was to test this particular prediction. The experiment was with three-, four-,

Table 8.1   Design of first conservation experiment

Pre-test judgement	Transformation judgement	Post-test judgement
A		A
	A–B	
B		B
	A–C	
C		C

five-, and six-year-old children, and its design is summarized in Table 8.1. The experiment, as this table shows, involved three separate sessions. In the first the children were simply shown the A, B and C displays separately over a series of trials in each of which they had to judge which of the display's two rows was the more numerous. These, then, were 'baseline sessions' in which we established with each child how well he normally did when each of the three displays was presented on its own. It was the second, and intervening, session which was the crucial one since this involved a perceptual transformation from one display to another. There were two transformations (though every child was given several examples of each) and both started with an A display, the display on which young children are normally right. One transformation was from A to B, the other from A to C. In both cases the child was shown A first and then watched the experimenter changing the appearance of the two rows until they looked like either B or C.

The reason for comparing these two transformations was that the

A–B transformation involved conflict, while the A–C transformation did not. The judgements typical of A and of B are quite the opposite of one another, and so conflict. No such conflict, as we have seen, exists in the A–C transformation. It follows that the conflict hypothesis predicts that the children would transfer information from the A to the

Table 8.2 First conservation experiment. Mean scores on A, B, and C displays (A–B, A–C)

			Pre-test	Exp. session	Post-test
Three-year group	A	$\bar{X}$	7·13		7·40
		SD	0·88		0·88
	B	$\bar{X}$	1·40	0·90	0·80
		SD	2·06	1·26	1·38
	C	$\bar{X}$	4·10	6·70	3·50
		SD	1·26	1·53	1·45
Four-year group	A	$\bar{X}$	7·07		7·33
		SD	1·06		0·69
	B	$\bar{X}$	1·60	1·20	1·70
		SD	1·82	1·83	1·73
	C	$\bar{X}$	3·40	7·00	4·10
		SD	1·93	0·97	1·37
Five-year group	A	$\bar{X}$	7·27		7·40
		SD	0·68		0·31
	B	$\bar{X}$	0·66	1·53	0·53
		SD	1·30	1·22	1·02
	C	$\bar{X}$	4·40	6·53	3·80
		SD	1·89	1·09	1·25
Six-year group	A	$\bar{X}$	7·33		7·47
		SD	0·69		0·72
	B	$\bar{X}$	0·87	1·27	1·20
		SD	1·75	2·14	1·68
	C	$\bar{X}$	4·20	7·27	3·67
		SD	1·45	1·06	1·40

(Exp. session scores are for B or C after transformation from A).

C display, where no conflict is involved, but not from the A to the B display since this plainly is a transformation which involves conflict.

The experimental results supported this prediction. They are shown in Table 8.2. In the two baseline sessions the children were consistently above chance-level with A, below chance level with B and around chance level with C. In the middle session they showed no sign of transfer across the perceptual change involved in the A–B transformation. Their performance on B was quite as bad in this session as in the two baseline sessions. However, in the other transformation they definitely did transfer information over the perceptual change. Their performance on C which was only random in the two baseline sessions was well above chance-level after the transformations from A in the middle session. It seems then that children could transfer the relative information about which row was the more numerous across a transformation to a display which would not on its own have produced the correct judgement. So they must be able to understand that the perceptual transformation has not actually altered the numbers of counters involved. Children only fail to transfer information across the transformation when the first and the second judgements are in conflict with one another. This, however, is not surprising, since the very fact

Table 8.3   Design of second conservation experiment

Pre-test judgement	Transformation judgement	Post-test judgement
A		A
	B–A	
B		B
	B–C	
C		C

that children use the length cue consistently demonstrates that they have no way of telling which is better, their A or their B judgement.

This basic point that young children have no way of knowing that their A judgements are sounder than their B judgements led to a second experiment. If children think that both sorts of judgements are equally good they should transfer information from B in exactly the same way as they do from A. They should transfer their B judgement, an incorrect judgement, when there is no conflict but not when there is a conflict with the second display.

The experiment which tested this idea (Bryant, 1972b, Exp. 2) was exactly the same as the first experiment except that the transformations in the middle session were from B, the display to which the child normally makes the wrong response. The experiment was again with three-, four-, five- and six-year-olds and the design as Table 8.3 shows consisted of two baseline sessions and a middle session in which there were two types of transformations, from B to A and from B to C. If children transfer the B judgement, which is the wrong judgement, they should do worse on A and on C in the middle session than in the two baseline sessions.

The pattern of results in this experiment was actually very similar

Table 8.4 Second conservation experiment. Mean correct on A, B, and C displays (B–A, B–C)

			Pre-test	Exp. session	Post-test
Three years	A	$\bar{X}$	7·19	6·81	7·25
		SD	0·90	1·00	0·90
	B	$\bar{X}$	1·19		0·81
		SD	1·13		1·07
	C	$\bar{X}$	3·38	1·56	4·38
		SD	1·41	1·41	1·05
Four years	A	$\bar{X}$	6·69	6·63	6·93
		SD	0·81	1·22	0·90
	B	$\bar{X}$	0·63		0·63
		SD	0·63		0·52
	C	$\bar{X}$	4·31	1·19	3·13
		SD	1·10	0·73	0·99
Five years	A	$\bar{X}$	7·38	7·44	7·15
		SD	0·93	1·17	0·56
	B	$\bar{X}$	0·38		1·00
		SD	0·48		1·06
	C	$\bar{X}$	3·44	0·63	4·00
		SD	1·77	0·86	1·84
Six years	A	$\bar{X}$	7·31	7·13	7·56
		SD	1·04	1·45	0·70
	B	$\bar{X}$	0·88		0·56
		SD	1·05		0·79
	C	$\bar{X}$	3·13	0·81	4·19
		SD	1·69	1·07	1·55

(Exp. session scores for A and C are after transformation from B).

to that of the first experiment. They are shown in Table 8.4. There was transfer to C in the B–C transformation but not to A in the B–A transformation. The children's answers to the question about C in the B–C transformation were well below chance-level, in that they usually selected the wrong row. Yet in the baseline sessions the children answered randomly when they were given the C displays. This means that the children were transferring the wrong response from B in the

B–C transformation and were transferring it as readily and as effectively as they transferred the correct response from A in the A–C transformation. On the other hand they did not transfer anything from B in the B–A transformation since their performance on A was at the same high level in all three sessions. Once again the children transferred a relative judgement to a display which would not on its own produce this judgement, and thus showed that they can use the invariance principle. Once again they do not show any transfer when the judgements which they normally make to the pre- and post-transformation displays are in conflict. They simply adopt the judgements which they would normally give to the more recent of the two displays.

Now it may be argued, and indeed it has been argued (Wallace, 1972), that these conclusions are not too different from some of Piaget's more recent suggestions. For example, in one recent paper Piaget (1968) does actually say that he now believes that the young child has a basic and innate understanding of invariance but that this understanding is overcome by perceptual factors in the conservation problem. Young children, according to this recent analysis, normally believe that perceptual alterations do not change the numbers of counters in a row. However, when children actually see a row being lengthened, this perceptual change overwhelms their belief in invariance, and they think that the number of counters really has changed. Applying this argument to the results of the experiments which have just been described, Piaget would say that the child uses his basic sense of invariance in the A–C and the B–C transformations, but that in the A–B and the B–A transformations the child actually thinks that the numbers in the changed rows have altered.

One can say two things about this. The first is that it is quite different from the conflict hypothesis which states that the child never thinks that perceptual transformations alter number. The second point is that the experiments which have just been described do not rule out this recent watered-down version of the invariance hypothesis. However, this hypothesis can be ruled out by other experiments which involve training children and which offer a very clear way of distinguishing between the conflict and the invariance hypotheses.

Training and the conflict hypothesis

There is a large literature on experimental attempts to teach 'conservation', that is, to train young children to make less errors in the conservation task. Most of these attempts have been concerned with ways of teaching the child the invariance principle. I shall not review these experiments, but instead I shall concentrate on experiments which look at the effects of training a child that some cues for number comparisons are correct and others incorrect.

The conflict hypothesis states that the young child makes errors in the conservation problem because he does not know that length is a bad cue and one-to-one correspondence a good cue. This means that teaching the child that one-to-one correspondence judgements are more reliable than length judgements without telling him anything about invariance should give him all the experience he needs to solve the conservation problem.

There are two experiments which test this prediction, the first by Gelman (1969) the second by Bryant (1972b, Exp. 3). Gelman's experiment was set up to examine not a conflict hypothesis but an attentional analysis of the conservation task. However, Gelman's methods, which are ingenious, are very relevant to the conflict hypothesis. Her experiment was with children aged between four and six years, and it involved three stages, a pre-test with conservation problems, a training period, and finally a post-test again with conservation problems. The most important of these was the middle period, when the children were trained, and the point to notice is that the training only involved showing the child about the right cues to use for number judgements. Her training procedure involved no transformations and therefore could have taught the child nothing about the invariance principle.

Gelman's experimental group was given a series of training trials, in each of which they were shown three quantities (either numbers of counters or lengths of straight lines) and had to say which was the odd one out. Some of the number displays which Gelman used in the training trials are shown in Fig. 8.3. After the child had made his choice about one display he was given 'feedback' which simply means that he was told whether he was right or wrong. Then he was given another display and was again given feedback about his choice, and trial followed trial until the child began to be correct all the time.

Notice that the child could only be right every time with the number displays when he learned to stop using the length cue, because if he used length as a basis for responding he would make the wrong choice with displays 2, 4, and 5 in Fig. 8.3, and this means that he would be wrong half the time. On the other hand the child is being taught nothing directly about invariance.

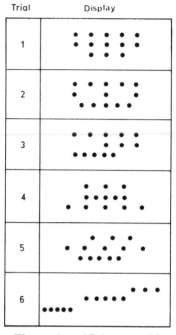

Figure 8.3   (Gelman, 1969)

This simple training procedure had an effect. The children who were trained in this way did much better on the traditional number conservation task after the training than before. Children who as a control were given the same displays but without feedback, and other children who were given oddity problems but with irrelevant material, were no better in the post-test than they were in the pre-test conservation problems. This is clear evidence indeed that children who are taught the right and the wrong cues for number judgements manage to solve the conservation problem, and this certainly suggests that the young child's difficulty with the conservation task is not a difficulty in understanding invariance but in knowing which of two judgements is the better one. Gelman's procedure helps the child resolve this difficulty by training him not to respond to the irrelevant cue of length to judge number.

The only possible objection to Gelman's experiment is that it shows the child that he should not rely on length without at the same time showing him why the length cue is unreliable. This is not an objection to the design of the experiment itself, which seems to be quite watertight. Nevertheless, one ought to consider real life, and it is quite probable that when in due course the child learns that the length cue is a thoroughly bad one he does so for some reason. One possible reason is that he eventually realizes that when he uses the length cue his judgements are liable to be very inconsistent over time. We looked into this suggestion in another experiment (Bryant, 1972, Exp. 3).

The aim of this experiment was to see what happens when young children are shown that their judgements are likely to be most unreliable when they use the length cue, and also that their one-to-one correspondence judgements are quite reliable. It is very easy to show the child that the B cue (length) is much less reliable than the A cue (one-to-one correspondence). All that one needs to do is to have several displays with which the child would usually employ the length cue

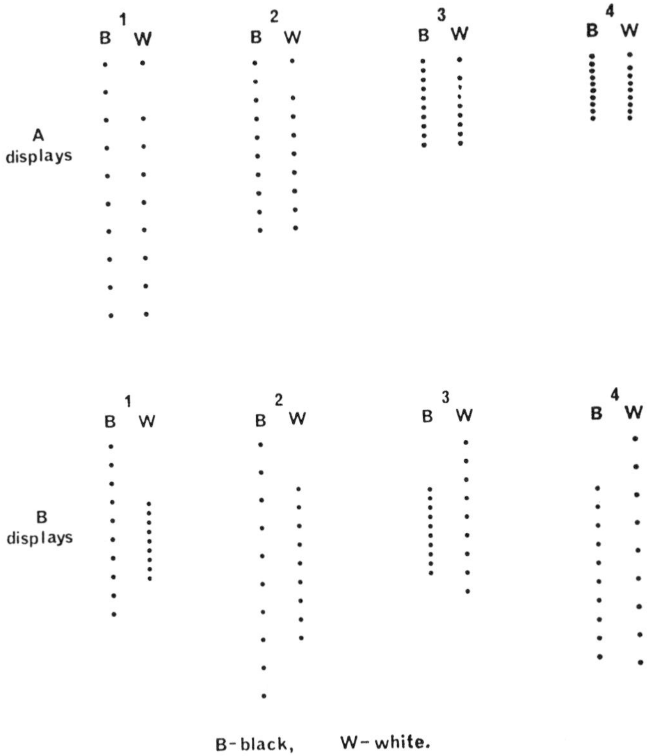

B-black,   W-white.

Figure 8.4

and transform them into each other, arranging things so that the row which is actually longer changes from display to display.

Consider the eight displays in Fig. 8.4. Each display contains a black and white row and there are different numbers of counters in the two rows. In this example there are always 10 in the black and 9 in the white rows. Four of the displays are characterized by the one-to-one correspondence cue (the A displays) and four by the length cue (the B displays).

Suppose that the child was shown one of the B displays and this was then transformed into another of the B displays and this in turn into another B display and so on over many transformations, in such a way that he sees all four displays many times. Each time he sees a display he is asked to judge which row has more counters in it. If he uses the length

Table 8.5 Design of the training experiment

	Pre-test judgement	Training trials	Post-test judgement
Experiment Group	A–B B–A	A_1–A_2–A_3–A_4 B_1–B_2–B_3–B_4	A–B B–A
Control Group	A–B B–A	A_1–A_2–A_3–A_4 B_1–B_2– OR B_3–B_4	A–B B–A

cue, as one must suppose he will, his judgements will be very inconsistent indeed. Half the time he will say that the black row is the more numerous and half the time that the white row is.

On the other hand, if he watches one A display being transformed into another A display and this into another A display and so on, his judgements over all these transformations should be entirely consistent. These displays are characterized by the one-to-one correspondence cue which will consistently tell the child quite correctly that the black row is the more numerous one. Thus transforming A displays into each other might demonstrate to the young child that the one-to-one correspondence cue is entirely reliable, just as transforming the B displays into each other will show him that the length cue is unreliable.

This, basically, was the training procedure adopted in our experiment. The design of the experiment is summarized in Table 8.5. The experiment was a three stage one with a pre-test, a training period and then finally a post-test. In the pre- and post-tests the children who were four and five years old were given the two conflict displays A–B and B–A (using the material described in Fig. 8.2) which caused such difficulty in our previous experiments (Bryant, 1972, Exps. 1 and 2). In the intervening training period which lasted for two sessions the children were given both A trials and B trials.

In the A trials they were shown a long series of A displays which they saw being transformed into one another. They had to say with each display which row was the more numerous, and their judgements were highly consistent from display to display. These children were given exactly the same kind of experience in the B trials, except that it was the B displays which they saw transformed into one another, and as a result their judgements about which row had more counters tended to change from display to display. So the experimental group was shown that their judgements tend to be reliable when they use the A cue and unreliable when they use the B cue.

There was also a control group who were given exactly the same treatment except that they were only shown B displays in which the length cue always led to the same judgement. They were always given B displays in which the longer row was always the same colour (black for some and white for others). Thus B judgements made by the control group would be as consistent as their A judgements. So both experimental and control groups were given ample experience with A and B displays, but only the experimental group was shown that the A cue was very much more reliable than the B cue.

The results of this experiment were positive. They are shown in Table 8.6. The crucial question was what would happen in the A–B trials in the post-test, since it is with the A–B transformation that the child normally dismisses the correct information from the A display in favour of the incorrect information from the more recent B display. What happened was that the experimental group made this type of error very consistently in the pre-test and then did better in the A–B trials in the post-test. The improvement was by no means perfect, but it was significant, and it did not occur in the control group. Once again we find that training a child that length is an incorrect cue will improve his performance in a conservation-type task.

However, these results do not just tell us that a child can be taught how to resolve the conflict between judgements which is inherent in the traditional conservation procedure. They also show us something about the child's understanding of invariance. We have seen that the crucial factor in this experiment was whether or not the child had prolonged

Table 8.6 Training experiment. Mean number correct post transformation scores

		Experimental group				Control group	
			Before training	After training			Before training	After training
Four-year group	B–A	$\bar{X}$	7·40	7·60	B–A	$\bar{X}$	7·20	7·30
		SD	0·80	0·66		SD	0·98	1·00
	A–B	$\bar{X}$	1·70	4·60	A–B	$\bar{X}$	0·80	0·90
		SD	1·10	3·04		SD	1·12	1·22
Five-year group	B–A	$\bar{X}$	7·40	6·90	B–A	$\bar{X}$	7·20	7·90
		SD	0·80	1·00		SD	0·75	0·30
	A–B	$\bar{X}$	1·10	4·30	A–B	$\bar{X}$	1·20	1·70
		SD	1·22	1·22		SD	1·20	1·19

experience of changing his judgements with the series of B displays. The decisive experience involves judging black to be the more numerous in one display, and then after seeing the black row bunched up and the white row spread out, saying that the white row is the one with more counters. It seems that this sort of experience eventually teaches children that the length cue is invalid. This conclusion has two important implications.

The first is that it rules out even the watered down hypothesis about invariance which states that the child generally understands and expects invariance, but that he is swamped by perceptual cues when he sees the length of a row changed and really thinks that this spatial rearrangement has altered the number of counters. If this hypothesis were correct then the child would simply think that the number of counters in the two rows was constantly changing in the B training trials, and so his experiences in these B trials should not bother him. But they obviously do have an effect, since it is these experiences which lead the children in the experimental group to change the way in which they react to a traditional conservation problem. The effect shows that the child is not swamped by perceptual cues. He realizes that the number has not changed and is perturbed at having to change his mind so often.

The second point is that it is just possible that in real life the young child eventually learns that the length cue is a bad one for number through the sorts of experiences which the children in the experimental group were given in the B trials. It may be that the child's experiences in his normal environment eventually show him that judgements based on length are most unreliable. Simple behaviour such as sharing sweets with a friend is likely to go completely and very obviously wrong when children try to use as incorrect a cue as length. However, as we shall see later, there are other possible ways in which a child could eventually learn that the length cue should not be used in number judgements.

However, whether or not the training procedures in this or in Gelman's experiment reflect the actual reasons why the normal child eventually manages to solve the traditional conservation problem, these two experiments do throw considerable doubt on theories which claim that young children do not understand invariance. We can conclude that the major reason for failures in the conservation problem may be the conflict between two incompatible judgements which must be part of the problem and which the young child can have no means of resolving in any other than a totally arbitrary way. It seems that the young child changes his judgement in conservation experiments not because he thinks that making a row longer changes its number, but because he cannot work out whether his first or his second judgement is the better one.

This, however, is not the end of the story. The evidence for the conflict hypothesis looks good, but the hypothesis itself throws up a rather disturbing paradox. We shall deal with this paradox in the next section, which will show that in one way, though in a manner very different from Piaget's original suggestion, the child's reactions to perceptual transformations really are very illogical and inconsistent.

Transforming a single quantity

The paradox in the conflict theory is this. The theory states that the child uses length as a cue for number in one situation and yet ignores it in another. He consistently judges that the longer of two simultaneously presented rows is the more numerous, but he does not think that making a single row longer increases its number. This would be quite inconsistent, and so the conflict theory must do two things. First it must establish clearly and directly that this paradox does occur, and that children who use the length cue when they compare two rows do not use it when they see the length of an individual row altered. Secondly, it must explain why children behave in this way. The first of these tasks turns out to be much easier than the second.

The traditional conservation task is no help in trying to sort out exactly when the young child uses the length cue. This is because the experiment involves both kinds of length cue. The child sees a single row lengthened, and he also has to make a judgement between two simultaneously presented rows whose lengths are different. Thus one cannot work out from this experiment whether the child who uses the length cue, uses it only between two simultaneously presented rows, or also thinks that the lengthened row has changed its number.

The problem is easily solved. All that is needed is a simple experiment with two conditions. In one condition the child is shown two rows of counters whose numbers are the same but whose lengths are different, and must say whether there is the same number of counters in each row or whether one has more than the other. In the other condition the child is shown one row only which is then either lengthened or shortened, whereupon he is asked whether or not the number of counters in the row is the same as it was before. If the child uses length as a cue for comparing the relative numbers of two different rows, as he usually does, he will say in the first condition that the longer of the two rows is the more numerous. If he also thinks that changing the length of a single row alters its number he will judge in the second condition that lengthening the row makes it more numerous, and shortening it, less numerous. According to the conflict theory the child should use the length cue in the first two-row condition but not in the second single-row one. He should judge that the longer of two different rows is the more numerous in the first condition but should still think that changing the length of the single row in the second condition does not alter the number of counters in it.

The condition which is new here is the second one in which the child sees only one quantity which is then transformed. Fortunately several recent experiments on the child's understanding of number have included a task of this sort. It was Elkind (1967) who originally suggested that young children should be given tasks in which they had to make judgements about a single quantity which they saw being transformed. Elkind's reasons for making this suggestion were different from mine, as we shall see, but the results of the experiments which follow his suggestion are relevant to the central paradox of my conflict theory.

We can concentrate on one of these experiments, which was conducted by Elkind and Schoenfield (1972) with young children of four and six years. The experiment involved other quantities as well as number; but their methods were exactly the same whatever the quantity, and I shall describe only the number problems. There were two of these. In one the child was shown one row only of five pennies, and told to look at it carefully. Then it was spread out and the child who had seen this change happening was asked whether there were 'more, less or the same number of pennies' as before. The other number problem was a traditional conservation task, in which the child first compared two equal rows of pennies arranged side by side in a one-to-one way, and then after one of these rows was spread out was asked to compare them again.

There are two points to notice about the results of this experiment. The first is that even the four-year-olds made hardly any errors in the first of these tasks which involved only one row of counters. Secondly, the four-year-olds made many more errors in the other type of task which involved two quantities. On the other hand, the six-year-olds made nearly as few errors in this latter task as they did when they were shown only one quantity.

This is an extremely exciting result, because it is the first exception that we have found to the very pervasive pattern of four-year-olds treating length as equivalent to number. When a single row is lengthened, they do not treat the change in length as a change in number.

One should mention briefly here that this point is not the one which interested Elkind and Schoenfield. Their argument was that the task which involves one row is an 'identity' task which tests the child's understanding of invariance without requiring him to make a transitive inference. On the other hand, the traditional task which they call the 'equivalence' task does involve an inference. Their conclusion is that the child understands invariance before he can incorporate information about the invariance of a particular quantity in an inference. It is certainly true that the new task avoids an inference which the traditional task does not: but this is almost certainly not the reason for young children's errors in the traditional problem, because as we saw in Chapter 3 young children of four years are perfectly capable of making transitive inferences.

In fact, Elkind and Schoenfield's control task, which was the traditional conservation problem, was too complex, because it differed from the experimental task, which involved a single quantity, in two ways. First the control task involved two quantities, not one, and secondly it required a transitive inference which the single quantity condition avoided. Therefore the experiment does not tell us which factor makes the control problem the more difficult one. However, one can at least guess that the inference possibility is the less plausible one, since there is evidence that young children can make inferences. If one rules out the effects of the child having to make an inference, then the only remaining possibility is that young children are entirely inconsistent in the way they use the length cue. They use it to compare two different and simultaneously presented rows, but they do not apply it to a row whose length they see being changed.

One can test this idea by using a different control task. Here the experimental task is the same as Elkind and Schoenfield's, but the control task is simpler. It involves no transformation and no inference. All that the child has to do is to compare two rows whose lengths are different despite the fact that their numbers are equal. Thus the experimental task tests whether young children use the length cue in deciding whether a single row whose length has changed has kept the same number of counters; and the control task tests whether they employ the length cue when they have to compare the number of counters in two different rows.

There is, however, one other difference between experimental and control conditions besides the fact that the experimental comparison is between a single row before and after a transformation, and the control comparison is between two different rows. The experimental comparison is a successive one while the control comparison is simultaneous. If the child uses the length cue in the simultaneous control condition, but not in the successive experimental condition, could he not simply have forgotten in the successive comparison what the actual length of the single row was before the perceptual transformation? After all we have established that young children are not very good at remembering absolute sizes.

One can take two precautions against the difference between the two conditions being the result of a memory lapse. One is simply to include a successive comparison between two different rows. If the child always uses the length cue to compare two different rows he should do so as much when the two rows are presented successively as when they are presented together. The other precaution is to introduce markers in all the successive comparisons. These markers could be crosses drawn on the piece of cardboard on which the counters are placed. In the experimental comparison which involves the transformation of a single row, there is the same number of crosses as counters and each counter is first put on one of these crosses. When the row is transformed and its length changed it is also moved slightly to the side. The child can now see the present length, and has a record of the past length of the row. Similarly, in the successive control comparison, one row is put on the crosses and then taken off them, and then another row distinguished by its colour, and of a different length, is laid out alongside the crosses. If both these precautions are taken, one can be quite sure that any consistent differences between the experimental and control comparisons have nothing to do with memory.

We introduced these precautions in a recent experiment (Bryant and Martin, unpublished material), with four-year-old children, to whom we gave three comparisons with several trials to each type of comparison. The first comparison was the experimental one in which we simply showed each child a single row and then either lengthened or shortened it, leaving markers to show its previous length. The child was asked

Table 8.7 Mean correct choices in the experiment on the transformation of a single row

		Single row transformed in length	Two rows of diff. length (successive)	Two rows of diff. length (simult.)
4 yr	Mean	6·35	3·70	2·85
	SD	2·35	2·43	2·70
5 yr	Mean	6·80	1·95	3·60
	SD	2·21	2·56	3·99

whether the row's number had changed or not. The second comparison was a successive control comparison between two different rows. We showed the child one row which was either red or green, and then took it away leaving markers to show how long a row it had been. Then we laid out a different row, coloured differently and a different length, alongside these markers. The child had to judge whether the two rows had the same number or not. The third comparison was a simultaneous control in which the child was shown two different rows of different lengths – one red the other green – alongside each other. Again the child had to judge whether the two rows had the same number or not.

The results of this experiment are given in Table 8.7. The children did well in the experimental condition and poorly in the two control conditions. Their scores were well above chance-level when they had to judge what had happened to the single row which had been transformed, and well below chance-level when they had to compare two different rows whose lengths were different but whose numbers were the same, and this second kind of comparison was done as poorly in a successive version as in a simultaneous one. Thus here for the first time we have direct evidence for the paradox suggested by the conflict hypothesis.

So the paradox exists and one can only guess at why it does exist. It seems that children have two rules, and use them in different situations. One rule is that number is invariant unless something is added or taken away. The other is that if two different rows have different lengths the longer one is usually the more numerous. They do not realize that these rules are inconsistent, and they apply the first rule when they see a quantity transformed, and the second when they have to compare different rows. How they acquire these different rules, when and how they learn that they are inconsistent, are questions which will have to be answered in future experiments.

Nonetheless, we have come some way on from Binet's original suggestion that the codes young children adopt for number are 'gross and defective'. We know now that they are defective in at least three different ways. First, they are relative and yet are not appropriate for inferences through the normal perceptual framework. Secondly, they are often wrong. Thirdly, they are often inconsistent: the length cue is inconsistent with the one-to-one correspondence cue, and the length cue itself is used inconsistently.

All of these deficiencies can be traced back to the fact that children initially use relative codes for number. When they acquire an effective absolute code they do not need a framework, they will find out how irrelevant is the length cue and they will rid themselves of their various inconsistencies. How this development takes place should surely be the central concern for future research in this area.

9

Vision and touch

So far we have dealt only with the visual information which the child has about his world. No doubt this is the most important perceptual information the child has about things around him. But it is not his only information, since he hears, feels, tastes and smells things as well.

One of the most interesting things about the fact that we perceive the world through several modalities is that the information coming from two modalities about the same thing is often equivalent. Perhaps the best example of this 'cross-modal' equivalence is between vision and touch. If someone holds a circular object it will produce a quite distinctive tactual impression, and if he looks at it it will produce a similarly distinctive visual impression. The tactual and visual impressions are equivalent in that any other shape will produce a different tactual and visual impression. It is theoretically possible to state exactly what any shape will look like merely by feeling it and vice versa.

We know that adults and even quite young children are aware of this visual-tactual equivalence and can use it to solve 'cross-modal' problems where they have to recognize the visual equivalent of an object that has been put in their hands. As we shall see, even a four-year-old child who is given an object with straight lines to hold can point out its visual equivalent from a visual choice of a straight and a curved line figure. He has some internal mechanism which to some extent can translate a tactual input into its equivalent visual input, and vice versa.

We can call this mechanism the 'cross-modal dictionary'. It is a dictionary because it translates the experience from one modality into the equivalent experience from another, in much the same way as a French-English dictionary translates a French word into its English equivalent. But simply to call the mechanism a dictionary only tells us about the job it does. It does not tell us how it works or develops.

The development of the cross-modal dictionary in young children is important from the point of view of the discussion in earlier chapters because it raises the absolute–relative question.

A cross-modal dictionary, whatever form it takes, must be able to connect particular entries from one modality with those from another, and whether the child uses absolute or relative codes is a factor which must affect its nature. If the child primarily uses relative codes the entries connected must be relative ones, which will mean that the cross-modal dictionary itself will suffer from many of the limitations characteristic of relative perception.

Indeed, it can be argued that cross-modal perception will be much more vulnerable to these limitations than perception within a modality. We can take as an example the perception of orientation. Suppose that the child is either shown two small parallel rods or feels them with one hand, and that he is asked whether their orientation is the same or not. We already know from the evidence presented in Chapter 4 that he can solve the visual problem with ease simply by noting whether the rods are parallel or not, and it is very likely that the child will solve the tactual problem successfully in the same relative manner. Relations of this sort between simultaneously presented lines are easily coded within a modality because both lines are presented together, making it possible to note whether the lines' orientations are the same without having to bother about what absolute orientations are involved.

However, a simple relative judgement like this is out of the question in a cross-modal version of this task, in which the child sees one of the rods and feels the other. Since the rods are thus presented in isolation from one another, the child must take in something about their absolute orientations before he can make a connexion between them. He has to use an absolute code to solve the cross-modal orientation comparisons for exactly the same reason that he has to take in absolute values to solve a successive, within-modal comparison.

So to solve this particular cross-modal problem the entries to the cross-modal dictionary will have to be couched in absolute terms, and the child who has no absolute code at his disposal will not be able to compare the orientation of the singly presented lines across modalities. If my analysis is correct, young children given the problems outlined above should be able to solve the within-modal comparisons with ease, and yet should have great difficulty when they have to compare orientation across modalities.

I am not suggesting that it is a universal law that children will be bound to make more errors in cross-modal than in within-modal tasks.

Cross-modal problems should only be more difficult when, as in the example given above, they can only be solved by absolute entries to the dictionary. If the problem can be solved by relative entries from each modality, the child should be able to make comparisons as easily across different modalities as within them.

This can be easily illustrated by another imaginary experiment. Suppose that the child is shown two rods which are parallel and that he feels two other rods which either are or are not parallel to each other. His task is to judge whether the two rods which he holds are arranged in the same way as the two rods which he sees. This cross-modal comparison could be solved by a relative, parallel/non-parallel code, and indeed so could any other cross-modal problem in which the stimuli differed in shape of pattern.

Thus the absolute–relative question should affect different cross-modal problems in different ways. If this analysis is correct it will not be a simple matter of cross-modal tasks being more difficult than within-modal tasks, or of cross-modal abilities developing more slowly than within-modal ones. Everything will depend on the task itself and, in particular, on whether the cross-modal and the equivalent within-modal problems can both be solved by a relative code or not.

This is a novel approach to the question of cross-modal abilities in children. Many psychologists have suggested that young children will have difficulty in making comparisons across different modalities. However, they have tended to use the term 'cross-modal' in a blanket manner, and have not tried to analyse which cross-modal comparisons will be relatively easy for young children and which difficult.

Yet these other approaches have produced some very interesting evidence, some of which supports the absolute–relative analysis of cross-modal development. I shall describe two of the main attempts to show that cross-modal abilities in general improve as children grow older before I go on to deal in detail with the absolute–relative approach to the problem. The first of these attempts is based on the idea that the cross-modal dictionary depends primarily on language and thus that the more words a child knows the greater will be his ability to connect things across modalities. The second is the suggestion that the central nervous system initially deals with the different modalities separately, but gradually, as the child grows older, integrates the different sources of information in a more and more co-ordinated way.

The language hypothesis

The language hypothesis is disarmingly simple. When I see a ball I have a distinctive visual experience to which I have learned to attach the verbal label 'ball'. I also have a distinctive tactual impression when I hold a ball, and again I have learned to attach the same verbal label 'ball' to that experience. So I attach the same verbal label to a visual and to a tactual experience, and then, because they have the same verbal label, I associate these two different perceptual experiences. Language then is a *tertium quid*, which serves as the connecting link between the two entries to the cross-modal dictionary. To use the analogy of the French-English dictionary once again, it is as though someone were able to connect a particular French with a particular English word only by knowing the Spanish equivalents of both.

The suggestion that language and cross-modal development are closely linked has been made at various times by Ettlinger (1967) O'Connor and Hermelin (1963) and Blank and Bridger (1964). It is fair to note, however, that in all three cases the suggestion was made in an extremely tentative manner.

This hypothesis produces three main predictions. The first, already mentioned, is that as children learn more words they will be able to make more comparisons across modalities. The second is that animals will not be able to make cross-modal comparisons because they do not speak, and the third, very similarly, is that human infants will not be able to recognize objects across modalities before they learn words, which begins to happen during their second year.

Of these three predictions, the first happens also to be the main prediction of the integration hypothesis, which is to be discussed later, and I shall then deal with the vexed question of whether or not there really is such a thing as cross-modal development in childhood. This eaves the two predictions about animals and human infants, who have no language and therefore should not be able to recognize objects across modalities.

Studies on animals

How can one test whether animals can recognize equivalent stimuli across modalities ? Broadly speaking, there are two kinds of test, cross-modal transfer and cross-modal matching experiments.

The cross-modal transfer experiments test whether a discrimination which is learned in one modality can be transferred to another. So if animals are trained to choose a square rather than a circle when these shapes are presented visually and cannot be felt, the question these experiments ask is whether they will continue to respond to the square when these same shapes are given them in the dark, and can only be distinguished tactually.

In the transfer experiment the visual and tactual presentations are separate. The animal is given first a visual and then a tactual task or vice versa. In the typical cross-modal matching experiment, on the other hand, the information from the two modalities is presented simultaneously. A standard stimulus is presented in one modality and two or more choice stimuli in the other. The animal must choose which matches the standard.

We have evidence about how animals manage both kinds of task and the most striking thing about that evidence is how poor the performance tends to be. Indeed, until quite recently one might reasonably have concluded that animals have no cross-modal ability at all, a conclusion of course which supports the language hypothesis.

This negative trend is particularly marked in experiments on cross-modal transfer, where some sensitive and carefully designed studies have demonstrated how difficult it is even for animals as sophisticated as monkeys to take advantage of cross-modal equivalence on a transfer task. The question of design is particularly important in these transfer experiments because one has to take great care to ensure that any transfer which one finds is genuinely cross-modal and is not caused by some non-specific factor such as the animal becoming more accustomed to the apparatus being used in the experiment.

Suppose, for example, that one gives all one's animals one discrimination and that half the animals learn it first visually and then tactually, the other half first tactually then visually. One might find that the animals who are given the visual discrimination second learn it faster than those who are given it first, and also that the animals who are given the tactual discrimination second learn it faster than those who are given it first. This pattern indicates transfer, because if the animals are consistently better in the second task than in the first they must be transferring something from the first to the second task. However, the transfer need not be cross-modal. It could be simply that the animals are getting more used to learning discriminations and that they are less frightened of the experimental situation. They could for this non-specific reason do better in the second task than in the first.

This difficulty was originally pointed out by Ettlinger who also devised some ingenious ways around it. In one experiment with monkeys (1961) he controlled the effects of non-specific transfer by making each learn two different discriminations in the transfer period. Half the animals were first given one discrimination, X, visually and then in the transfer period were given a completely new visual discrimination, Y, visually. The other animals were first given the Y discrimination tactually and then in the transfer period had to learn it again visually: but in the same period they were given discrimination X, a new one for them, tactually. Thus in the transfer period each group is given a discrimination which it already learned in another modality, and which the other group is learning in the transfer period for the first time. If the animals do transfer information about shape cross-modally, they should in the transfer period learn the discrimination which they were previously given in the other modality much faster than the group who are being given the same task for the first time.

There was no sign of cross-modal transfer in this experiment. Nor did monkeys do any better in another experiment on cross-modal transfer by Blakemore and Ettlinger (1966) which introduced a different kind of control for non-specific transfer. They taught monkeys a tactual discrimination and then gave the same animals the same stimuli visually. However, although half the animals had to learn the same discrimination as before, for the other half the discrimination was reversed, so that the correct solution in the visual task was the incorrect solution in the tactual task and vice versa. Then all the animals were given exactly the same tactual discrimination as they started with. If monkeys transfer information across vision and touch, one would expect those for whom the solution was the same in all three stages to learn much faster in the second and third stage than the animals for whom the solution was reversed in the intervening visual period. However, there was no reliable sign of any difference at all between the two groups. Thus one must conclude that here again the monkeys failed to take advantage of cross-modal equivalence in a transfer problem.

There seems to be no good reason for disagreeing with Ettlinger's conclusion that monkeys might be incapable of cross-modal transfer in the sense in which the term is used in cross-modal transfer studies. Certainly it seems that where positive trends have occurred in transfer experiments on monkeys, as in an experiment by Wilson and Shaffer (1963), these trends have turned out to be unreliable (Ettlinger, 1967). However, one cannot conclude from animals' failure in these experiments that they are completely incapable of recognizing objects across modalities. Transfer experiments are quite complex. For example, they involve memory. It may be that the animal is perfectly capable of recognizing a visible square as the equivalent of a tactual square when the two are presented together, but that his memory of a visual square is such that it cannot be translated into its tactual equivalent. The obvious test of this notion is a simultaneous cross-modal matching task.

Matching experiments are much more difficult with monkeys than with four-year-old children. Whereas the child can be instructed how to match and can then get on with the experiment, a monkey must, in one way or another, be trained to match. But how do you train a monkey to match without, at the same time, teaching it the solution to the matching problem?

Ettlinger and Blakemore (1967) also devised an ingenious solution to this problem in another series of experiments on monkeys. In one experiment all the animals were given three shapes on every trial, one of which was a tactual, standard shape which they could not see and the other two were the visual choice shapes which they could not feel. The two visual shapes (a door knob and a lid) were the same on every trial, but one tactual standard was presented on half the trials and another on the other half. Half the animals formed an experimental group and were given a 'true' matching task. For them the tactual and visual shapes corresponded. The tactual standards were also a door knob and a lid and these animals had to learn that when the tactual standard which they could feel but not see was a doorknob they would be rewarded for reaching for the visual doorknob, and when the tactual standard was a lid the correct visual choice was also the lid.

The experimental group learned this task quite satisfactorily. They were able in the end to choose the visual shape which was identical to the standard. However, as Ettlinger and Blakemore pointed out, this success, on its own, does not necessarily mean anything about the recognition of shape across modalities. It could simply be the result of a form of learning which is often described as 'conditional learning'. The animals may have learned that they had to go to the visual stimulus A when they felt the tactual stimulus A, without realizing that tactual A and visual A were in any way equivalent. The control, which the experimenters introduced against this conditional learning, was a 'false' matching task.

In this 'false' task the other half of the animals were given the same visual shapes (the doorknob and the lid) but quite unrelated tactual shapes (a cylinder and an irregular shape). The animals had to learn to choose the doorknob when one of these tactual shapes was the standard and the lid when the other was the standard. They could only solve this task on a conditional basis by learning to associate each visual shape with a tactual standard. This they achieved, which means that they can learn to associate particular tactual with particular visual stimuli. However, what is more interesting is that they learned the control task as rapidly as the experimental group learned the true matching task, which strongly suggests that the experimental group was not aware of the fact that the tactual and the visual shapes were equivalent. The experimenters correctly concluded that their monkeys had not been able to match shapes across the two modalities.

Yet there is more to be said about this interesting experiment, because it raises a most provocative paradox. It is true that it shows that the monkeys were not able to take advantage of the equivalence of identical visual and tactual shapes. However, it also shows that they are very well able to learn to associate particular visual experiences with particular tactual experiences. Both the control and the experimental groups could apparently bring together visual and tactual experience in this way. The fact that they can manage this sort of association across modalities raises a most interesting question.

If they can learn in the course of the experiment to associate two visual shapes with two tactual shapes, why do they not learn in their normal life to associate the tactual experience which they have of particular shapes with the visual experience which typically accompanies it ? After all, one can quite plausibly suggest that all that is necessary for an animal or a human to build up a cross-modal dictionary is the ability to learn to associate visual and tactual experiences. So the results of Ettlinger and Blakemore's experiment suggest both that monkeys do not have a cross-modal dictionary, and yet that they do have the mechanism for associating visual with tactual experience, which might well be both a necessary and sufficient condition for acquiring the dictionary.

This is certainly a paradox, but one can think of ways of resolving it. One possibility is that the shapes which were given to the experimental animals were so unfamiliar that they were outside the range of the cross-modal dictionary. It is quite possible that the monkeys had never handled shapes which were anything like doorknobs and lids. In fact, once they are captured, monkeys that are used in psychological experiments tend to live in an environment where there is not much to handle. These monkeys may have had a cross-modal dictionary which could deal with the shapes they had been accustomed to see and handle, but which could not deal with unfamiliar shapes whose visual and tactual correlates they had never had a chance to put together. Thus one can conclude from Ettlinger and Blakemore's experiment that there is a possibility that monkeys have the ability to acquire a cross-modal dictionary, but that the circumstances in which they are kept restrict its range.

The results of another, more recent, matching experiment support the idea that some higher animals possess a cross-modal dictionary and can use it. This experiment by Davenport and Rogers (1970) was with chimpanzees and orang-utans. These are animals which, in many ways, are more sophisticated than the monkeys tested in Ettlinger's experiments. Nonetheless, any evidence about their ability to make direct cross-modal judgements is relevant to the language hypothesis. Throughout this experiment these animals were given two tactual shapes and one visual shape on each trial. The visual shape was the standard and it was always identical to one of the two tactual choices. The experiment was divided into three stages. The first simply accustomed the animals to making a choice between two tactual objects. In the second stage, which lasted between 1000 and 2500 trials, the animals were taught to match cross-modally with a limited number of stimuli. By the end of this stage the animals could match the visual standard with the correct tactual choice on more than 80 per cent of the trials. Of course, their eventual success in this stage may again only have been another instance of conditional learning. However, in the third stage quite new shapes (unfortunately not specified in the experimenters' account) were given to the animals over 40 trials, with different shapes being used on each trial. The three animals who were given these last cross-modal matching problems all performed at a level well above chance. They could, therefore, match visual shapes with their tactual equivalents.

Here then is evidence of a cross-modal dictionary in animals. One is still left with some interesting questions. How would monkeys manage in Davenport and Rogers' task? Would chimpanzees succeed in a cross-modal transfer problem? Nonetheless, we have at least an answer to the question with which this section started. Some animals can recognize some objects across different modalities without the help of language. The extreme form of the language hypothesis is no longer tenable.

Cross-modal studies of human infants

The discovery that some animals have a cross-modal dictionary at their disposal makes it seem more likely that humans might also be able to recognize objects cross-modally before they can describe the objects in words. Until quite recently, we had no direct evidence on this question. It is true that Blank, Altman and Bridger (1968) have claimed to have shown that three-year-old children can transfer information about shapes, for which they do not have a proper name, across modalities. However, evidence about children as old as this, children who can talk quite well, is bound to be ambiguous. There is no way that one can rule out the possibility that they attached their own idiosyncratic verbal labels to the shapes which they had to discriminate. Obviously, the most direct data can only come from experiments with children who are too young to have any language.

In some ways infants as young as this pose an even more awkward problem than animals to the experimenter who is concerned with cross-modal abilities. One cannot tell infants to match objects because they will not understand instructions, and one cannot really train them to match, because this would be a long and complex business. It would be quite impossible to maintain the baby's interest, which is volatile at the best of times, for such a long period. What is needed is a matching task which could be given in a cross-modal version, which does not involve verbal instructions and which is short enough not to lose the baby's attention.

Recently, we managed to devise such a task (Bryant, Jones, Claxton, and Perkins, 1972). This was based on the simple observation that babies are attracted to and usually reach for objects which they have heard make a noise. This simple fact makes two things possible. First, one can use the child's attraction to noisy objects as the basis of a simple within-modal matching task. We devised a matching task with babies aged between six and twelve months in which we used the two pairs of shapes which are shown in Fig. 9.1, each baby being given one pair only. Our procedure involved three stages. In the first stage we showed the two objects to the child, who was sitting on his mother's lap, by putting them on the table in front of him, but out of his reach. We removed them, and then in the second stage put one of the objects back in front of the infant and made it make a noise. Each object contained inside it a bleeper activated by a mercury switch: the single object was put on the table in the second stage, and tilted slightly. This set off the switch which in turn started the bleeper. Then this object was removed, and finally in the third stage both objects were replaced on the table, but this time within the child's reach. We recorded which of the two objects the child touched first. Our argument was that if the

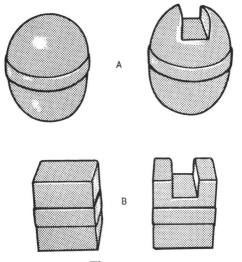

Figure 9.1

babies consistently reached in the third stage for the object which had previously made a noise they would have demonstrated that they really do like noisy objects and also that they are able to make a visual match.

The results of our first experiment demonstrated that both these things are true. We gave 30 infants, all of them less than twelve months, pair A and another 30 pair B, and we arranged matters so that each of the objects in each pair was the 'noisy' one for an equal number of infants. We found that 23 of the 30 given pair A and 22 of the 30 given pair B reached for the object which had previously made a noise. This result, of course, is well above chance level, and so we can conclude that we have found a simple, short and effective way of giving babies a matching task. Thus far the test is a within-modal one.

The second thing that the child's attraction to noisy objects makes possible is a cross-modal matching task which is quite suitable for babies. We demonstrated this in three experiments (Bryant *et al.*, 1972) in which the procedure was exactly the same as in the visual matching problem except that in the middle stage the noisy object was presented tactually. In the first experiment, the two objects were shown to the baby as before. They were removed, and in the second stage the experimenter took one of the objects concealed in her hand over to the baby. She took one of the baby's hands in her other hand and placed it on the shape, at the same time encircling the baby's hand with her own. While the baby touched the object the experimenter made it bleep. Then she removed the object and in the third stage placed it on the table in full view of the baby together with the other object. Thus the child only had tactual information to tell him which was the noisy object, and the question was whether he could use this tactual information when he was shown the two objects visually in the third stage. To be able to reach for the object which they had previously felt, the babies would have to link tactual with visual information.

The results of these three cross-modal experiments were consistently positive. In all of them we demonstrated that infants of less than twelve months have some cross-modal ability. In the first experiment out of the 30 infants to whom we gave pair A 23 reached in the third stage for the object which they had previously felt and had made a noise: 30 infants were given pair B but only 19 of these reached for the previously felt object. The first result is significantly higher than chance while the second is not.

This first experiment involved only one experimenter and to check its reliability we then did a second experiment which involved two experimenters and a 'blind' procedure. One experimenter managed the visual presentation in the first and third stages while the other gave the babies the 'noisy' object to hold in the intervening second stage. The experimenter who was responsible for the visual presentations never knew when she gave the babies the choice in the final stage which of the two objects was the 'correct' one. The results of this cross-modal experiment were almost identical to those of the first. Again they were positive with pair A, with which 24 out of 31 babies reached for the object which they had felt before, but were still at chance level with pair B with which only 18 out of 30 infants reached for the 'correct' object. Finally, in the third cross-modal experiment we repeated the blind procedure with the successful pair A only, this time with two different experimenters. The results were again significant: 21 out of 30 infants reached for the object which they had felt before.

Here, then, for the first time is a clear demonstration of a cross-modal dictionary in children who are too young to speak. Exactly what features they do connect across modalities when they solve the cross-modal discrimination involved in pair A is not clear. It may be that they simply note that one figure has only curved lines, while the other has straight lines as well as curved lines. Certainly this would help to account for the babies' failure with the other pair, since here the figures involved straight lines only. This question can only be sorted out by other experiments with a variety of stimuli to establish which cross-modal discriminations are possible and which impossible for babies of this age.

We can be sure, however, that the pre-verbal infant has some kind of a cross-modal dictionary even if we do not yet know its exact form, and this conclusion has several important implications. One obvious point is that the extreme form of the language hypothesis about cross-modal organization is no longer tenable. These experiments taken together with the work on chimpanzees and orang-utans show quite clearly that cross-modal links are possible without the help of language.

Another equally important point is that the discovery of cross-modal organization in babies is relevant to many of the questions which have been raised about early conceptual development. Piaget, for example, suggested that up to the age of roughly eight months the child is unable to grasp the fact that an object which disappears from his view goes on existing (Piaget, 1954). According to Piaget the fact that babies as young as this do not reach out and search for objects which they have seen being put behind some cover or other demonstrates that they think that once the object disappears from view it ceases to exist. This may be so: but our discovery of cross-modal recognition in groups of babies whose mean ages were always less than nine months shows that at least in some situations babies do have a mechanism which could tell them that an object which has disappeared still goes on existing. Suppose that a baby looks at an object which is in his hand and then moves his hand so that, although he is still holding the object, he can no longer see it. If now he can recognize the shape which he holds as equivalent to the shape which he saw before it disappeared he has an effective way of understanding that the object still exists, despite the fact that he can no longer see it.

A third and final point is that we are now faced with a new question, which is simply whether there is cross-modal development at all. If babies can recognize shapes as equivalent across vision and touch, is it not possible that cross-modal abilities are built in and do not have to improve or increase as the child grows older? This is a rather complex question, since one can mean quite different things by the phrase 'cross-modal development'. Perhaps the most convenient approach to this problem is to consider the integration hypothesis, because its basic point is that children's ability to bring together information from different modalities increases with age.

The integration hypothesis

What does cross-modal development mean? One thing that is certain is that it means something quite different from within-modal development. These two kinds of development must be very firmly distinguished.

Suppose, for example, that one finds, as indeed one commonly does, that younger children make many more errors than older children when they have to say which of two visual choices is the same as a tactual standard or vice versa. There is certainly some improvement with age in cross-modal performance here, but the reasons for the developmental change are ambiguous.

There are two possible reasons. One is simply that the perceptual information which comes from one or both of the modalities is faulty; in other words the younger child could be making many errors simply because he is unable, for example, to discriminate shapes tactually. This is a failure within a modality. The other possible reason is a cross-modal one. The child may err because although he receives perfectly discriminable information, he cannot connect it cross-modally. It follows that either within-modal or cross-modal development could be responsible for improvement with age.

So one has to add some kind of control task to ensure that the older children's usual superiority on a cross-modal problem really does indicate cross-modal development. The control is simply to include within-modal as well as cross-modal matching problems. In the cross-modal problems the standard is presented visually and the choices tactually, or vice versa. In the within-modal problem the standard and the choices are either all presented visually or all tactually. Thus the within-modal problems test the child's ability to distinguish things tactually and visually while the cross-modal problems also test their ability to associate tactual and visual information.

Two patterns must emerge from an experiment like this if one is to be sure that it does demonstrate the existence of cross-modal development. First, the performance certainly of the younger groups (and sometimes also of the older groups) must be consistently worse in the cross-modal than in the within-modal problems. Secondly, the discrepancy between cross- and within-modal conditions must decline with age.

The first requirement is both obvious and important. If, for example, the younger children make as many errors when standard and choices are all tactual, as in the cross-modal problems, then all their errors on the cross-modal tasks could be explained away as tactual failures. This would mean that any improvement with age on this task would have nothing to do with cross-modal ability.

The second requirement is not so obvious, but at least as important. If there is such a thing as cross-modal development the difference between the child's performance on cross- and within-modal problems must diminish with age. Suppose one found, for example, that both a five- and an eight-year-old group made more errors on cross-modal problems than on within-modal problems, and that not only were the older children generally better, but that their superiority was as great in the within- as in the cross-modal tasks. This would mean that the discrepancy between cross- and within-modal tasks was the same for both age groups; it would also mean that the superiority of the older children in the cross-modal task could be explained in terms of within-modal improvement. They could simply be getting better at the cross-modal task because the information which they were receiving from one or both of the modalities concerned was becoming that much clearer. Thus one must also establish that as they get older the rate at which they improve in the cross-modal problem is different, and faster, than their rate of improvement in the within-modal problems.

I have described these two requirements in some detail because they have been neglected by many of those who have tried to show that there really is such a thing as cross-modal development. Several psychologists have put this suggestion forward. The clearest and in some ways the most influential example can be found in the two monographs written by Birch and Lefford (1963, 1967). They suggested the hypothesis that initially children tend to treat the different modalities separately and that a major feature of the perceptual development of children is a marked increase in 'intersensory organization'. Birch and Lefford also argued that this development might influence other important activities such as the way a child learns to read and to write.

Their experiments were with children aged from five to eleven years and they simply presented these children with cross-modal problems. The children were given pairs of shapes, one shape presented in one modality, the other in another, and they had to judge whether the two shapes were the same or different. This is one form of a cross-modal matching problem. Three modalities were involved, vision, touch (which was called the haptic modality) and kinaesthesis, which meant that the child had to hold a stylus which was moved around the figure's contours. There were thus three cross-modal problems: these were visual-haptic, visual-kinaesthetic and haptic-kinaesthetic.

The children's performance in all three kinds of problem improved with age, and the improvement was most marked in the two conditions which involved the kinaesthetic modality. The authors concluded that they had demonstrated that intersensory organization increases with age. But this conclusion is obviously based on inadequate evidence. The experiment included no within-modal controls and it is therefore quite impossible to work out whether the improvement was a within-modal or a cross-modal one.

Much the same criticism can be made about three other developmental studies which include only cross-modal tasks. Blank and Bridger (1964, Exp. 1), Conners, Schuette, and Goldman (1967), and Abravanel (1968) all found that older children did better than younger children in cross-modal matching tasks, and wrongly concluded that this demonstrated the existence of cross-modal development. All of these studies leave the question of cross-modal development quite open.

What about studies which do include the correct controls? These produce a very different picture. One of the first studies in this field by Hermelin and O'Connor (1961) included all the necessary within-modal controls (which makes it rather surprising that so many other subsequent experiments omitted them) and showed that the children aged between four and seven and a half years made as many errors in the two within-modal (visual–visual and tactual–tactual) conditions as in cross-modal problems. Obviously there is no sign here of cross-modal development.

Nor was there any specifically cross-modal development in another study by Rudel and Teuber (1964) with children of four and five years, who had to match shapes cross-modally (visual–tactual and tactual–visual) and within-modally (visual–visual and tactual–tactual). Here the older children were better than the younger children, but they were better in all four kinds of problem. Moreover, the tactual–tactual condition was actually harder than either of the two cross-modal conditions for both age groups, and the improvements which occurred with age were as great in the within-modal as in the cross-modal tasks. Thus these results fail to fulfil either of the two requirements for cross-modal development, and Rudel and Teuber rightly concluded that their data provided no support for the idea of cross-modal development.

Many more recent cross-modal experiments seem to lead to the same conclusion. One of our cross-modal experiments (Milner and Bryant, 1970) was with children of five, six, and seven years who had to judge whether pairs of shapes were the same or not. The tactual–tactual condition was again harder than either of the cross-modal tasks, and the difference between age groups was as great in the difficult tactual within-modal task as it was in either of the two cross-modal tasks. Other experiments, too, have confirmed that children find it no harder to compare shapes across vision and touch than to compare them tactually (Millar, 1971; Rose, Blank and Bridger, 1972).

These experiments all involved shape. There is, however, some indication that cross-modal development might be easier to demonstrate when children have to deal with differences in length. Connolly and Jones (1970) made children of five, eight, and eleven years, as well as adults, compare the lengths of lines cross-modally and within-modally, and found that the children generally performed worse in the cross-modal than in the within-modal tasks, and also that there was a general improvement with age. They concluded that this showed that there is some cross-modal development when lengths have to be compared.

However, even this conclusion can be questioned. The results, it is true, conform to the first requirement in that the cross-modal performance is worse than within-modal performance. But what about the second requirement that the difference between cross-modal and within-modal performance should diminish with age? Connolly and Jones did not actually consider this question. However, the scores definitely do seem to suggest that between the ages of five and eight years the children improve more in cross-modal than in within-modal tasks. So it may indeed be the case that the ability to compare lengths cross-modally improves as children grow older.

Thus there may be a discrepancy between shape and size. Children's major difficulty with shapes is in distinguishing them on the basis of touch. As soon as children can recognize shapes by touch they are also able to translate this tactual information into its visual equivalent and vice versa. With length, however, it may be that children's cross-modal performance initially lags behind their within-modal performance and that this lag itself grows smaller as children grow older.

If this analysis is correct the integration hypothesis put forward by Birch and Lefford must be wrong. The hypothesis, which itself is based on data about shape discrimination, cannot explain the consistent failure of properly designed experiments to discover any sign of any specifically cross-modal improvement in children's ability to recognize shapes. Nor can it explain the apparent difference between cross-modal experiments with shape and with length. Obviously any account of children's cross-modal abilities must tackle this discrepancy. One possible approach to this particular problem, as well as to the whole question of children's cross-modal ability, is in terms of absolute and relative codes.

Absolute and relative codes and the cross-modal question

Most of this book has been concerned with continua such as size, orientation, position, and number. With these continua one can specify quite precisely the absolute value of any particular stimulus, and also its exact relation to any other stimulus along the continuum. Shape is not a continuum of this sort. One cannot give shapes absolute values, and it is hard to specify exactly what the relations between different shapes are. Perhaps the most important thing to realize about the dimension of shape is that, as the Gestalt psychologists so often demonstrated, each shape constitutes a set of relations. A triangle consists of three lines in a certain relation to each other and provided that these relations stay constant the shape made by these lines will always be the same. This means that showing a child a single line on its own and asking him to take in its length is quite different from showing him a single triangle and asking him to take in its shape. To the length of the line he must respond absolutely, whereas he only has to take in the relations of the lines which make up the shape.

This difference between shape and other continua such as size ought to have some effect on children's performance in cross-modal experiments, because it means that the child can solve cross-modal problems about shape with a relative code, but that he needs an absolute code to deal with cross-modal length problems.

This is one way of explaining the discrepancy between length and shape. The idea is, of course, very speculative and one needs a great deal more experimental evidence before one can take it at all seriously. In particular, we need to know a lot more about how children deal with recognizable continua such as size, length, orientation, position, and even number in cross-modal problems If my analysis is right, it should be quite easy to find other instances where cross-modal problems are more difficult than within-modal problems with continua such as these.

Nevertheless, the young child's consistent success with cross-modal comparisons of shape, and his apparent difficulties with cross-modal length comparisons, provide a reasonable starting point for the hypothesis that the crucial factor which is most likely to determine how the child manages a cross-modal problem is whether it demands an absolute or a relative code.

IO

Experiments

There were two main aims to this book. One was to put forward a theory about some aspects of perceptual and conceptual development, and the other to consider the various ways in which experiments might help us understand children's behaviour. In this final chapter I shall concentrate on the second question.

The reason for emphasizing the experiments rather than the theory is simply that, if this book makes any lasting contribution, this will most probably take the form of making people think about how to do experiments with children properly and about the exact value of these experiments. My theory, though it has the value of linking a whole set of experiments which are normally treated quite separately, is almost certainly wrong. At this stage in the development of developmental psychology any theory can hope at best only to be an approximation to the truth.

This is not a pessimistic statement. Perhaps the sanest way to treat theories in developmental psychology is to think of them as stepping stones. Someone's theory provokes someone else to do some further experiments, which produce a new theory which is a closer approximation to the truth than the first, and so on.

It is wrong then to think that an incorrect theory has contributed nothing or to suggest that a new theory overthrows an old one. The new and the old are essentially part of the same process and make their contribution to the understanding of children's behaviour in the same way. It would be quite wrong, for example, to suggest that criticisms of Piaget's use of evidence in the traditional transitivity and conservation procedures overthrow his theory or diminish its contribution in any way at all. Our experiments on both these problems could not have been conceived had Piaget not posed the questions and produced his experiments in the first place.

On the other hand, some of the points which have been made about experiments may have a significance which reaches well beyond the specific studies discussed in this book. It should be clear that it is quite difficult to pin down a definite point about children's behaviour using the experimental method. Many examples have been given of studies in which the experimenters' conclusions about their data have turned out to be unjustified. Why does this happen so often in experimental studies of young children?

The main difficulty seems to lie in the use of age as a variable. Many psychologists have been content to find a simple age difference and to base their very specific conclusions on this one difference. This is almost always unjustified because one task will involve various aspects of behaviour and the age difference could mean a change in one or more of these. Almost always one needs an added control task which is similar to the experimental task in all ways *except* the aspect under inspection. If an age difference is found in performance on the experimental task but not on the control task, the experimenter can then begin to conclude something specific about development. Experiments on specific developmental changes should look for an interaction between age and tasks (experimental *and* control) and not just an age difference in a single task.

This point is illustrated very clearly by the examples of some of the experiments on transitive inferences and on cross-modal organization. The traditional transitivity experiments involved asking children of different ages one question only, the inferential AC question, and finding that older children answered this question better than younger ones. Yet answering the AC question involves at least two different aspects of the task: making an inference and remembering the information that A > B and that B > C. Therefore the age difference on the AC question could be a difference in making inferences or in remembering. The essential control is to ask the child to recall also the answer to AB and BC. Only if younger and older children remember the direct AB and BC comparisons equally well, and the older children still do better on the inferential AC question, is it permissible to conclude that there is an age difference in the ability to make inferences.

The cross-modal example is very similar. It is quite impermissible simply to give children cross-modal tasks, to find that younger children are worse on them than older children and to conclude from this a development in cross-modal ability. The cross-modal tasks involve so many other factors – for example, getting the information through the individual modalities concerned. Therefore, the age difference in the cross-modal task could indicate either a cross-modal or a within-modal difference. Again, we need a control task which, in this case, is a within-modal one. This point about interaction and developmental research is a simple and, in some ways, an obvious one. Yet it is often ignored, and this is probably one of the main reasons why much experimental work in development is ambiguous. We can wonder, however, whether this is the only problem. Recently, the experimental approach has been quite severely criticized for a number of reasons. One can take, for example, Tinbergen's criticisms (in the introduction to a recent book edited by Blurton-Jones, 1972) about the use of experimental methods to study children's behaviour. Other contributors to this book also expressed reservations about the experimental method.

The criticisms which are levelled against the experimental approach tend to take two forms. One form, often made by people who advocate the use of observation, is that experiments are artificial and have very little to do with real life. The other is that although experiments might tell us something about the child's immediate behaviour they explain very little about the causes of developmental change. I shall take these two criticisms separately and shall argue that the second is a great deal more worrying than the first.

Experiments and real life

Experiments take place in 'controlled circumstances'. The circumstances have to be controlled if the experimenter is to be sure that he is giving the same task every time in the same way, and that all irrelevant variables are excluded. But real life is not controlled and usually not so simple or aseptic as the typical experimental situation. Thus behaviour in one might have very little to do with behaviour in the other, and so perhaps we should abandon experiments and confine ourselves to observation of behaviour as it is typically behaved.

There is something, but not a lot, in this argument. Certainly observation is an extremely useful method which has produced a great deal of interesting information about children. The renewed enthusiasm for observation which comes from people interested in ethological studies of animal behaviour, who want to adapt the ethological approach to the study of young children, should produce fresh advances in this area. There can be no doubt that the observational approach is particularly well suited to the study of some kinds of behaviour, and conveniently the aspects of behaviour which respond especially well to the observational technique are often more or less impossible to study in an experimental situation. Two good examples are the way in which young children react to their mothers and the way in which they play. It is very difficult to think of ways of slotting either type of behaviour into an experiment without seriously disturbing them. Yet both are easily amenable to observation.

But what when – as often happens – simple observation does not solve a problem about behaviour? Take, for example, the common observation that children confuse letters like p and q or b and d when they begin to learn to read. These letters are mirror images, but is this the cause of the confusion? Simply observing children making the error will not answer this question. One has to take the behaviour apart in an experiment probably involving artificial figures which the child has never seen before and which in some cases are mirror images and in other cases not.

Of course the dilemma remains that the experimental manipulations are artificial. However, if the experimenter finds a promising solution to the question of why p is confused with q and b with d, he can then test his solution in a real situation. For example, it was suggested in Chapter 5, on the basis of experiments on children's reactions to quite artificial material, that such confusions between letters might have nothing to do with mirror-images but rather with the unavailability of appropriate framework cues. This hypothesis could be tested in a real life situation with real letters by introducing framework cues down a margin. If this test worked then one could be fairly sure that the experimental situations were relevant to the child's ordinary behaviour.

Thus in order to look at the potentially crucial variable this very satisfactory process moves from observation of a pattern of behaviour which could not itself be explained by simple observation, to experimental manipulations in a laboratory, and then back to real life. Fortunately, this process is often possible in the study of the way children perceive and understand things around them, because many of the problems are closely related to educational demands such as learning to read or to measure or to count and therefore one has a convenient and fairly systematic 'real' environment in which to test aspects of one's experimental hypotheses. Thus the problem of the artificiality of experiments, though it exists, need not be too much of a worry.

However, this is by no means all that should be said on this subject, since recently attempts have been made to suggest that while some experiments on a particular problem are arbitrary and artificial, others on the same problem are more representative of what goes on outside the laboratory. These suggestions should be treated with great care especially since there seems to be a tendency to suggest that the less well-designed experiment is the one which more accurately reflects real life.

For example, Piaget (1968) has suggested that experiments which produce more optimistic conclusions than his about children's logical abilities are tapping a lower level of behaviour – a level based on action – and that the children do not have a proper understanding of principles involved. There is nothing wrong with the suggestion that one should be careful about the level at which behaviour is organized. Whenever my four-month-old daughter sneezes she always seems to sneeze twice. I cannot conclude from this that she understands how to count up to two. However, in the cases which Piaget discusses it seems just as likely that the difference between his and other studies is not that they are tapping different levels but that they introduce different controls.

We can take as an example the experiment involving the conservation of weight. This was originally designed by Piaget and has essentially the same design as the number problem in that the child has first to compare two quantities in a form which makes him think them to be equal and then, after seeing one of the quantities perceptually transformed, compare them again. The only difference in the weight problem, apart from the fact that judgements are on the basis of weight, is that only two objects are involved, for example, two balls of clay. On the whole, children below the age of about ten years cannot solve this weight problem. They say that the quantities are equal before and unequal after the transformation.

Now since the basic design of this and of the traditional number problem are basically the same it follows that both will have the same weaknesses. Chapter 8 showed that the basic ambiguity in the conservation procedure arose from the fact that, although only one quantity was transformed, two quantities were involved. When children change their minds over a transformation this could be because of the way they normally judge the two quantities in each display and might have nothing to do with their understanding of invariance. A purer test of the understanding of invariance is to present only one quantity and to see what the child does when this is transformed. When this is done with number (Elkind and Schoenfield, 1972) young children perform much better than they do in the traditional problem when two numbers are involved.

Recently Mounoud and Bower (unpublished) have carried out an ingenious version of the weight conservation problem. They examined children's judgements of weight by measuring the amount of pressure exerted on each weight when the child gripped it. They also worked with one quantity at a time. They found convincing evidence that the young child understands that perceptually transforming something does not alter its weight. Children as young as eighteen months did not alter the pressure with which they gripped an object after they saw it transformed.

The study is a neat one, but Mounoud and Bower's conclusions from it are questionable. They argue that there are two levels in the understanding of invariance, one behavioural and the other conceptual. They suggest that their experiment taps the first of these, showing that the very young child can organize his behaviour around the assumption of invariance without being able to deal with the principle on a conceptual level. They agree with Piaget that his experiments demonstrate children's inability to understand the invariance of weight at a conceptual level before the age of ten.

They do not define these two levels very precisely and admit that the connexions between them are not yet clear. Perhaps the reason for this obscurity is that the behavioural–conceptual split does not really exist, and that the real difference between their procedure and that of Piaget was that theirs involved only one quantity and was the purer test, while Piaget's involved two quantities with all the consequent ambiguity. The difference between the two experiments is probably one of design and controls, and there are no real grounds for thinking that one experiment is more representative of a certain level of behaviour in real life than the other.

We can conclude that the question of the relevance of experiments with children to real life needs watching. Experiments may be less suitable for some problems than for others, but they can tell us something about the child's behaviour which other methods cannot. Moreover, it is extremely dangerous to maintain that some experiments are more representative of real life than others. The connexion between behaviour within and without the experiment should be checked in each individual case as far as it can be.

Experiments and the causes of developmental change

Developmental psychologists, broadly speaking, are concerned with two main questions. One is about what changes take place in children's behaviour as they grow older, the other about the causes of these developmental changes.

These questions are quite separable, as is demonstrated by the fact that, while experimental psychologists have been very good about producing evidence to answer the question of what developmental changes there are, they have been extremely inept when trying to answer the causal question. The reason is very simple. Experiments are suitable for sampling what behaviour is like at a particular point in time. It is very easy to put three- and five- and eight-year-old children through a comparable experimental situation and see how they differ. However, causes of developmental change are another matter. The actual changes do not take place in the laboratory. They take place outside, gradually and unpredictably. It is easy to identify them once they happen but difficult to see them actually happening. If the changes cannot be looked at as they occur, then the question of how to get at their causes is an awkward one.

Surprisingly, there has been very little discussion of this problem or even of the difference between discovering what the developmental changes are and what causes them. Nonetheless, one can discern at least two systematic ways in which psychologists have tried to get round the difficulties involved in the causal question. One is to induce the developmental change in the laboratory through training, and then to use the training as a model for what normally causes the change in real life. The other, more indirect, approach involves looking at the behaviour which has developed and trying to work out from its components how it must have been acquired. Both approaches have their weaknesses.

The main difficulty with the first approach is that one cannot be sure that the conditions which successfully produce the behavioural change in the laboratory are the same as those which ordinarily produce it in real life. This problem is most dramatically illustrated by the fact that it is often possible to simulate the same developmental change through a number of quite different manipulations. Conservation training procedures are an example. Two rather different training techniques, Gelman's and mine, both of which led to improvement in traditional conservation tasks, were described in Chapter 8. There have been other successful attempts to train 'conservation', using still other techniques. Thus different conditions can be made to cause the same change in behaviour, and which, if any, of them causes this change in real life remains a mystery. It would certainly be rash to conclude anything definite about causes from a training experiment.

On the whole, psychologists have preferred the other approach which involves an inference from the nature of the development about its causes. This also has its difficulties because it is usually impossible to be confident that the inference is correct.

A good example is Kuenne's hypothesis that children eventually manage to code relations through learning the correct relative words, like 'smaller' and 'larger'. Her evidence for this notion was that the children who succeeded in her relative task tended to be more fluent and to produce the relative words in a spontaneous way more frequently than the children who failed. It was shown in Chapter 2 how further evidence has demonstrated that her hypothesis is almost certainly wrong. But even without this further evidence one can conclude that the hypothesis is certainly inferential, and that the inference is an unsecured one. She has put together two facts about the older children (they succeed in her relative test and they are better verbally) and has concluded that it is the language which has led to the developmental change. However, there were many other differences between the older children who succeeded and the younger ones who did not. The older children have had more perceptual experience; they are taller; their motor skills are better; they have been to school longer. Any of these differences could also be cited as a causal factor if one used Kuenne's logic. Even if one could show that the developmental change was associated specifically with language, one could still not be certain that language was the causal agent. It could have been that a developing ability to code relations perceptually made it possible for the child to learn and to use the correct relative terms.

I have discussed Kuenne's inference about language as a cause of developmental change because her work was described earlier. However, exactly the same sort of criticism can be levelled against some of the more recent 'verbal mediation' theories about development (Bryant, 1971).

Thus both approaches to the question of causes of development tend to be unconvincing, and perhaps one has to face the fact that this is the weakest point in the experimental approach to children's behaviour. It is easy to show that the most direct experimental evidence offered for any theory about child development is always about what the developmental changes are and not about their causes. Certainly this is true of the theory described in this book, where very little indeed has been said about causes and even that has been speculation. It is true also of Piaget's theory. Take for example his idea of the pair of complementary mechanisms, assimilation and accommodation. The first involves the child taking in new information about his environment within the framework of his existing intellectual structures, and the second involves altering and reorganizing these structures when they are no longer accounting adequately for the new experiences which the child has as he grows older. These are interesting ideas, but very general, and as such difficult to pin down in any experiment. Not surprisingly Piaget does not offer any direct experimental evidence for assimilation and accommodation.

Is there any way round the difficulty which the experimenter has with causes of developmental change? Perhaps the best approach is to acknowledge the serious nature of the difficulty, but to point out that nonetheless experiments may be able to say something significant. There are two ways in which they might be able to do this.

One is that experiments have at least some significant negative value. One may have difficulty finding definite evidence for a causal hypothesis, but it is often very easy to produce convincing evidence against one. One example is our demonstration that babies can recognize some shapes across modalities long before they can speak (Bryant et al., 1972). This effectively rules out the hypothesis that children develop a cross-modal dictionary solely on the basis of having common words for equivalent visual and tactual experiences. Since it is at least as important to be able to eliminate hypotheses as it is to find evidence to support them, the value of this sort of negative information about causes should not be ignored.

Secondly, experiments might help to discover causes by testing more specific hypotheses. The difficulty with ideas like assimilation and accommodation has been that their status as general developmental principles has made them so abstract that they are very hard to identify in an experimental situation. But is there any need for these general principles? It may be that each specific change breeds the next one. Thus what actually causes a change may be different each time. Take measuring as a possible example of this process. We know that the ability to make spontaneous measurements is an important development in itself, but quite as important are its possible consequences. As soon as a child starts these spontaneous inferences he will be able to compare and to connect features of his environment which hitherto have been quite separate for him. This must change his view of the environment and could well lead to some further changes in behaviour. Thus we should consider not only what developmental changes occur but what their consequences are, and this might give us some fairly specific ideas about causes.

This more specific approach has the advantage of being open to experiment. It is much easier to think of the experiences which a child might have when he begins to measure things than of a tangible example of accommodation. One could test, without any preconceptions, what exactly are the effects of a prolonged bout of measurement. If the effects are anything like any developmental changes which occur at this stage then one could argue that it is probable that the child's measuring experiences are leading to further developmental changes.

The difference between adopting this approach and taking an arbitrary training technique as a model for the cause of a developmental change is that we already know that the child really does have experiences with measuring in real life, whereas we usually have no evidence that he has the sort of experiences which are given to him in a training procedure. Nevertheless, it must be admitted that this approach can still only lead to conclusions which are at best inferential. The causal question is still an extremely difficult one, and it is time that the problem was properly recognized by psychologists who work with children.

The strengths of the experimental approach

In spite of their limitations there are some things which experiments do very well. We have seen that they can take apart the various aspects involved in quite complex development. Experiments can also make another extremely valuable contribution to the study of children's behaviour, one which has been the central concern of this book. They can show how different aspects of behaviour which at first sight seem to be quite heterogeneous actually work in much the same way and are controlled by common factors. Thus we have seen a connexion between the way children remember orientation and their ability to make inferences, between the way they learn about number and the way they judge position, between the way they learn a size discrimination and the way they perform in a size constancy problem, between their ability to recognize objects cross-modally and the way they code relations. None of these connexions between different patterns of behaviour could have been made without experiments since it is only through experiments that one can work out, for example, that children use inferences through the framework as a basis for judging orientation, or that the spatial one-to-one correspondence cue, which children use in number comparisons, works on the same 'in-line' basis as do their judgements about position.

The more this kind of connexion can be made, the more economical and orderly will our theories about development be. One can extend these connexions still further. This book has stayed within the general area of perceptual and conceptual development. Yet these developments do not take place in isolation from social and emotional events. We can be fairly certain that some of the factors which affect the child's perception of his environment will also influence his emotional and social development. To extend outwards to these fields is the obvious next step. 'Only connect', as E. M. Foster urged, is surely excellent advice for developmental psychologists. A good way to begin making connexions is through experiments.

References

ABRAVANEL, E. (1968) The development of intersensory patterning. *Monogr. Soc. for Research in Child Development*, **38**, No. 118.

ALBERTS, E. and EHRENFREUND, D. (1951) Transposition in children as a function of age. *J. Exp. Psychol.*, **41**, 30–8.

BECKMANN, H. (1924) Die Entwicklung der Zahlleistung bei 2–6 jahrigen kindern. *Zeitschrift fur angewandte Psychol.*, **22**, 1–72.

BINET, A. (1890) La perception des longueurs et des nombres chez quelques petits enfants. *Revue Philosophique*, **30**, 68–81. (Trans. in POLLACK, R. H. and BRENNER, M. J. (eds.) (1969) *The Experimental Psychology of Alfred Binet*. New York: Springer.)

BIRCH, H. G. and LEFFORD, A. (1963) Intersensory development in children. *Monogr. Soc. for Research in Child Development*, **28**, No. 5.

BIRCH, H. G. and LEFFORD, A. (1967) Visual differentiation, intersensory integration and voluntary motor control. *Monogr. Soc. for Research in Child Development*, **32**, No. 2.

BLAKEMORE, C. B. and ETTLINGER, G. (1966) Cross modal transfer of conditional discrimination learning in the monkey. *Nature*, **210**, 117–18.

BLANK, M. and BRIDGER, W. H. (1964) Cross-modal transfer in nursery school children. *J. Comp. Physiol. Psychol.*, **58**, 277–82.

BLANK, M., ALTMAN, L. D., and BRIDGER, W. H. (1968) Cross-modal transfer of form discrimination in pre-school children. *Psychonom. Science*, **10**, 51–2.

BLURTON JONES, N. (ed.) (1972) *Ethological Studies of Child Behaviour*. Cambridge: Cambridge University Press.

BRAINE, M. S. (1959) The ontogeny of certain logical operations: Piaget's formulation examined by non-verbal methods. *Psychological Monograph*, **73**, No. 5, 1–43.

BRAINERD, C. J. (1973) The origin of number concepts. *Scientific American*, **228**, March.

BROWN, J. R. (1931) The perception of velocity. *Psychol. Forschung.*, **14**, 199–232.

BRUNER, J. S., OLVER, R. R., GREENFIELD, P. M. *et al.* (1966) *Studies in Cognitive Growth.* New York: John Wiley.

BRYANT, P. E. (1969) Perception and memory of the orientation of visually presented lines by children. *Nature*, **224**, 1331–2.

BRYANT, P. E. (1970) Perceptual learning in the severely subnormal. *Proc. 2nd Congress of Internat. Assoc. for Scientific Study of Mental Deficiency*, Warsaw.

BRYANT, P. E. (1971) Cognitive development. *Brit. Medical Bull.* (*Cognitive Psychol.*), **27**, 200–05.

BRYANT, P. E. (1972a) Inferences in perception. Paper presented to the Brit. Psych. Soc. London.

BRYANT, P. E. (1972b) The understanding of invariance by very young children. *Canad. J. Psychol.*, **26**, 78–96.

BRYANT, P. E. (1973) What the young child has to learn about logic. In HINDE, R. A. and J. S. (eds.), *Constraints on Learning.* London: Academic Press.

BRYANT, P. E. (1973) Discrimination of mirror images by young children. *J. Comp. Physiol. Psychol.*, **82**, 415–25.

BRYANT, P. E., JONES, P., CLAXTON, V. C., and PERKINS, G. M. (1972) Recognition of shapes across modalities by infants. *Nature*, **240**, 303–4.

BRYANT, P. E. and TRABASSO, T. (1971) Transitive inferences and memory in young children. *Nature*, **232**, 456–8.

COLE, M., GAY, J., GLICK, J. A., and SHARP, D. W. (1972) *The Cultural Context of Learning and Thinking.* London: Methuen.

CONNERS, G. R., SCHUETTE, C., and GOLDMAN, A. (1967) Informational analysis of intersensory communication in children of different social class. *Child Devel.*, **38**, 251–66.

CONNOLLY, K. and JONES, B. (1970) A developmental study of afferent–reafferent integration. *Brit. J. Psychol.*, **61**, 259–66.

CORBALLIS, M. C. and BEALE, I. L. (1970) Bilateral symmetry and behaviour. *Psychol. Review*, **77**, 451–61.

CORBALLIS, M. C. and BEALE, I. L. (1971) On telling left from right. *Scientific American*, **224**, March.

DAVENPORT, R. K. and ROGERS, C. M. (1970) Inter-modal equivalence of stimuli in apes. *Science*, **168**, 279–80.

DESCOEUDRES, A. (1921) *Le Développement de l'enfant de deux à sept ans.* Paris: Delachaux & Niestle.

DODWELL, P. C. (1962) Relation between the understanding of the logic of classes and of cardinal number in children. *Canad. J. Psychol.*, **16**, 152–60.

DONALDSON, M. and BALFOUR, G. (1968) Less is more: a study of early language comprehension. *Brit. J. Psychol.*, **59**, 461–71.

ELKIND, D. (1964) Discrimination, seriation and numeration of size. *J. Genet. Psychol.*, **104**, 275–96.

ELKIND, D. (1967) Piaget's conservation problems. *Child Devel.*, **38**, 15–27.

ELKIND, D. and SCHOENFIELD, E. (1972) Identity and equivalence at two age levels. *Develop. Psychol.*, **6**, 529–33.

ERIKSEN, C. W. and HAKE, H. W. (1955) Multidimensional stimulus differences and accuracy of information. *J. Exp. Psychol.*, **50**, 153–60.

ETTLINGER, G. (1961) Learning in two sense modalities. *Nature*, **191**, 308.

ETTLINGER, G. (1967) Analysis of cross-modal effects and their relationship to language. In MILLIKAN, C. H. and DARLEY, F. L. (eds.) *Brain Mechanisms Underlying Speech and Language*. New York: Grune & Stratton.

ETTLINGER, G. and BLAKEMORE, C. B. (1967) Cross-modal matching in the monkey. *Neuropsychologia*, **5**, 147–54.

FORGUS, R. H. (1966) *Perception*. New York: McGraw-Hill.

GELMAN, R. (1969) Conservation acquisition: a problem of learning to attend to relevant attributes. *J. Exp. Child. Psychol.*, **7**, 167–87.

GELMAN, R. (1972) The nature and development of early number concepts. In REESE, H. W. (ed.) *Advances in Child Development and Behaviour*, Vol. 7. New York: Academic Press.

GIBSON, E. J. (1969) *Principles of Perceptual Learning and Perceptual Development*. New York: Appleton Century Croft.

GIBSON, E. J., GIBSON, J. J., PICK, A. D., and OSSER, H. (1962) A developmental study of the discrimination of letter-like forms. *J. Comp. Physiol. Psychol.*, **55**, 897–906.

GILINSKY, A. S. (1955) The effect of attitude on size perception. *American Journ. Psychol.*, **68**, 173–92.

GRAHAM, F. K., ERNHART, C. B., CRAFT, M., and BERMAN, B. W. (1964) Learning of relative and absolute size concepts in preschool children. *J. Exp. Child Psychol.*, **1**, 26–36.

GRATCH, G. and LANDERS, W. F. (1971) Stage IV of Piaget's theory. *Child Devel.*, **42**, 359–72.

HAKE, H. W. and GARNER, W. R. (1951) The effect of presenting various numbers of discrete steps on scale reading accuracy. *J. Exp. Psychol.*, **42**, 358–66.

HELMHOLTZ, H. von (1866) *Treatise in Physiological Optics*, New York: Dover.

HELMHOLTZ, H. von (1873) The recent progress of the theory of vision. In *Popular Scientific Lectures*. New York: Appleton.

HELMHOLTZ, H. von (1894) The origin of the correct interpretation of our sensory impressions. *Zeitschrift fur Psychologie und Physiologie Sonnes*, 7, 81–96. (Trans. in WARREN, R. M. and R. P. (eds.) *Helmholtz on Perception*. New York: J. Wiley.)

HERMELIN, B. and O'CONNOR, N. (1961) Recognition of shapes by normal and subnormal children. *Brit. J. Psychol.*, **52**, 281–4.

HOWARD, I. and TEMPLETON, W. P. (1966) *Human Spatial Orientation*. New York: John Wiley.

HULL, C. L. (1943) *Principles of Behaviour*. New York: Appleton Century Crofts.

HUMPHREY, G. (1951) *Thinking: An Introduction to its experimental psychology*. London: Methuen.

HUTTENLOCHER, J. (1967a) Discrimination of figure orientation: effects of relative position. *J. Comp. Physiol. Psychol.*, **63**, 359–361.

HUTTENLOCHER, J. (1967b) Children's ability to orient and order objects. *Child Devel.*, **38**, 1169–76.

JEFFREY, W. E. (1958) Variables in early discrimination learning: I. Motor responses in the training of a left–right discrimination. *Child Devel.*, **29**, 269–75.

JOHNSON, R. C. and ZARA, R. C. (1960) Relational learning in young children. *J. Comp. Physiol. Psychol.*, **53**, 594–7.

KENDLER, T. S. (1950) An experimental investigation of transposition as a function of the difference between training and test stimuli. *J. Exp. Psychol.*, **40**, 552–62.

KENDLER, H. H. and KENDLER, T. S. (1956) Inferential behaviour in pre-school children. *J. Exp. Psychol.*, **51**, 311–14.

KENDLER, H. H. and KENDLER, T. S. (1961) Inferential behaviour in children, II. *J. Exp. Psychol.*, **61**, 422–8.

KENDLER, H. H. and KENDLER, T. S. (1967) Inferential behaviour in young children. In LIPSITT, L. P. and SPIKER, C. C. (eds.) *Advances in Child Development and Behaviour*, Vol. III.

KESSEN, W., HAITH, M. M., and SALAPATEK, P. H. (1970) Infancy. In MUSSEN, P. H. (ed.) *Carmichael's Manual of Child Psychology*, Vol. I. New York: John Wiley.

KLAHR, D. and WALLACE, J. G. (1973) Quantification processes in the development of concrete operations. Proc. XXth Internat. Congr. Psychol. Tokyo.

KLUVER, H. (1933) *Behavior Mechanisms in Monkeys*. Chicago: University of Chicago Press.

KOHLER, W. (1918) Simple structural functions in the chimpanzee's and in the chicken's representation. Reprinted in ELLIS, W. D. (1938) *A Sourcebook of Gestalt Psychology*. London: Routledge.

KUENNE, M. R. (1946) Experimental investigation of the relation of language to transposition behaviour in young children. *J. Exp. Psychol.*, **36**, 471–90.

LASHLEY, K. S. (1938) The mechanism of vision, XV: Preliminary studies of the rat's capacity for detail vision. *J. General Psychol.*, **18**, 123–93.

LAWRENSON, W. and BRYANT, P. E. (1972) Absolute and relative codes in young children. *J. Child Psychol. Psychiat.*, **13**, 25–35.

LIBERMAN, I. Y., SHANKWEILER, D., ORLANDO, C., HARRIS, K. S., and BERTI, F. B. (1972) Letter confusions and reversals of sequence in the beginning reader: Implications for Orton's theory of developmental dyslexia. *Cortex*, **8**, 128–42.

LUCHINS, A. S. and LUCHINS, E. H. (1970) Wertheimer's seminars revisited: problem solving and thinking. Albany, N.Y.: Faculty Student Assoc. State University at Albany.

MACH, E. (1959) *The Analysis of Sensations*. New York: Dover Press.

MACKINTOSH, N. J. and SUTHERLAND, N. S. (1963) Visual discrimination by the goldfish: the orientation of rectangles. *Animal Behav.*, **11**, 135–41.

MAIER, N. R. F. (1939) Qualitative differences in the learning of rats in a discrimination situation. *J. Comp. Psychol.*, **27**, 289–332.

MCCULLOCH, T. L. (1935) The selection of the intermediate in a series of weights by the white rat. *J. Comp. Psychol.*, **20**, 1–11.

MEYER, M. E. (1964) Discrimination learning under various combinations of discriminanda. *J. Comp. Physiol. Psychol.*, **58**, 146–147.

MILLAR, S. (1971) Visual and haptic cue utilisation by pre-school children: the recognition of visual and haptic stimuli presented separately and together. *J. Exp. Child Psychol.*, **12**, 88–94.

MILLER, G. A. (1956) The magical number seven plus or minus two: some limits on our capacity for processing information. *Psychol. Rev.*, **63**, 81–97.

MILNER, A. D. and BRYANT, P. E. (1970) Cross-modal matching by young children. *J. Comp. Physiol. Psychol.*, **71**, 453–8.

MOUNOUD, P. and BOWER, T. G. R. (1973) Conservation of weight in infants. Unpublished manuscript.

NEISSER, U. (1967) *Cognitive Psychology.* New York: Appleton Century Crofts.

O'CONNOR, N. and HERMELIN, B. M. (1963) *Speech and Thought in Severe Subnormality.* London: Pergamon Press.

ORTON, S. T. (1937) *Reading and Writing and Speech Problems in Children.* London: Chapman & Hall.

OVER, R. and OVER, J. (1967) Detection and recognition of mirror-image obliques by young children. *J. Comp. Physiol. Psychol.*, **64**, 467–70.

PIAGET, J. (1952) *The Child's Conception of Number.* London: Routledge & Kegan Paul.

PIAGET, J. (1953) *The Origins of Intelligence in the Child.* London: Routledge & Kegan Paul.

PIAGET, J. (1953) How children form mathematical concepts. *Scientific American*, November.

PIAGET, J. (1954) *The Construction of Reality in the Child.* London: Routledge & Kegan Paul.

PIAGET, J. (1968) Quantification, conservation and nativism. *Science*, **162**, 976–9.

PIAGET, J. (1969) *The Mechanisms of Perception.* London: Routledge & Kegan Paul.

PIAGET, J. (1970) *Genetic Epistemology.* New York: Columbia University Press.

PIAGET, J. and INHELDER, B. (1941) *Le Développement des quantités physiques chez l'enfant.* Paris: Delachaux & Niestle.

PIAGET, J. and INHELDER, B. (1956) *The Child's Conception of Space.* London: Routledge & Kegan Paul.

PIAGET, J., INHELDER, B., and SZEMINSKA, A. (1960) *The Child's Conception of Geometry.* London: Routledge & Kegan Paul.

POLLACK, I. (1952) The information of elementary auditory displays. *J. Acoustical Soc. of America*, **24**, 745–9.

REESE, H. W. (1968) *The Perception of Stimulus Relations*. New York: Academic Press.

RILEY, D. A. (1958) The nature of the effective stimulus in animal discrimination learning: transposition reconsidered. *Psych. Rev.*, **65,** 1–7.

RILEY, D. A. (1968) *Discrimination Learning*. Boston: Allyn & Bacon.

ROCK, I. (1970) Towards a cognitive theory of perceptual constancy. In GILGEN, A. R. (ed.) *Contemporary Scientific Psychology*. New York: Academic Press.

ROCK, I. and EBENHOLTZ, S. (1959) The relative determination of perceived size. *Psychol. Rev.* **66,** 387–401.

ROSE, S. C., BLANK, M. S., and BRIDGER, W. H. (1972) Intermodal and intramodal matching of visual and tactual information in young children. *Develop. Psychol.*, **6,** 482–6.

RUDEL, R. G. and TEUBER, H. L. (1963) Discrimination of the direction of line by young children. *J. Comp. Physiol. Psychol.*, **56,** 892–8.

RUDEL, R. G. and TEUBER, H. L. (1964) Cross-modal transfer of shape discrimination by children. *Neuropsychologia*, **2,** 1–18.

SHERMAN, M. B. and STRUNK, J. (1964) Transposition as a function of single vs. double discrimination training. *J. Comp. Physiol. Psychol.*, **58,** 449–50.

SIEGEL, J. A. and SIEGEL, W. (1972) Absolute judgment and paired associate learning: Kissing cousins or identical twins. *Psychol. Rev.* **79,** 300–16.

SMEDSLUND, J. (1963) The development of concrete transitivity of length in children. *Child Devel.*, **34,** 389–405.

SMEDSLUND, J. (1966) Performance on measurement and pseudo-measurement tasks by 5–7 year old children. *Scandinav. J. Psychol.*, **7,** 81–92.

SPENCE, K. W. (1937) The differential response in animals to stimuli varying within a single dimension. *Psychol. Rev.* **44,** 430–44.

SPENCE, K. W. (1938) 'Relative' vs 'absolute' size discrimination by chimpanzees. *Psychol. Bull.*, **35,** 505.

SUTHERLAND, N. S. (1957) Visual discrimination of orientation and shape by octopus. *Nature*, **179,** 11.

THOULESS, R. H. (1931a) Phenomenal regression to the real object. *Brit. J. Psychol.*, **21,** 339–59.

TINBERGEN, N. (1972) Foreword in BLURTON JONES, N. (ed.)

Ethological Studies of Child Behaviour. Cambridge: Cambridge University Press

VERNON, M. D. (1957) *Backwardness in Reading.* Cambridge: Cambridge University Press.

VERNON, M. D. (1971) *Reading and its Difficulties.* Cambridge: Cambridge University Press.

WALLACE, J. G. (1972) *Stages and Transition in Conceptual Development.* Slough: N.F.E.R.

WERTHEIMER, MAX (1912) Numbers and numerical concept in primitive peoples. Reprinted in ELLIS, W. D. (ed.) (1938) *A Sourcebook of Gestalt Psychology.* London: Routledge & Kegan Paul.

WERTHEIMER, MAX (1961) *Productive Thinking.* London: Tavistock Press.

WILSON, W. and SHAFFER, O. C. (1963) Inter-modality transfer of specific discrimination in the monkey. *Nature*, **197**, 107.

WITKIN, H. A. (1959) The perception of the upright. *Scientific American*, February.

WOHLWILL, J. F. (1960) Absolute vs relational discrimination on the dimension of number. *J. Genet. Psychol.*, **96**, 353–63.

WOHLWILL, J. F. (1963) The learning of absolute and relational number discriminations by children. *J. Genet. Psychol.*, **101**, 217–28.

WOODWORTH, R. S. and SCHLOSBERG, H. (1954) *Experimental Psychology.* London: Methuen.

YOUNISS, J. and MURRAY, J. P. (1970) Transitive inferences with non-transitive solutions controlled. *Devel. Psychol.*, **2**, 169–75.

ZEAMAN, D. and HOUSE, B. J. (1963) The role of attention in retardate discrimination learning. In ELLIS, N. R., (ed.) *Handbook of Mental Deficiency.* New York: McGraw-Hill.

Name Index

Subject Index